Family Dynasties

T0382766

A remarkable 15 Nordic family businesses are among the 500 biggest companies in the world and the Nordic countries have more dynasties than most others per capita and in GDP terms. The willingness, often reluctant, of both the political system and labour movement to accept asset accumulation has helped these Nordic businesses survive. The top 1% of Swedes own close to 25% of the country's wealth, as opposed to 16.5% of Spaniards, where dynasties are also abundant. The pattern has held a firm grip on the Nordic countries since the Industrial Revolution and emergence of free enterprise. The trend is particularly pronounced in comparison with the Anglo-Saxon countries—somewhat less so relative to places like Italy, Japan, Germany and South-Asian countries.

This book describes the factors and dynamics behind the ability of Nordic businesses to grow and thrive from one generation to the next in the process of becoming dynasties. Far from being commercial enterprises, they are a venue for power, philanthropy, passion, conflict, freedom and captivity. Like many other dynasties, the Nordic ones are a witch's brew of Machiavelli's Prince, Marx's belief in the potential of the meritocracy and Smith's baker who works to sustain his family—topped by a spoonful of Weber's Protestant Ethic.

This book will be key readings for students and scholars of entrepreneurship, corporate governance, business history, Scandinavian history, family business and enterprises and the related disciplines.

Hans Sjögren is a professor at Linköping University and Stockholm School of Economics, Sweden.

Routledge International Studies in Business History
Series editors: Jeffrey Fear and Christina Lubinski

For more information about this series, please visit: www.routledge.com

Family Dynasties

The Evolution of Global Business in Scandinavia

Hans Sjögren
Translated by Ken Schubert

LONDON AND NEW YORK

First published 2018 by Routledge

2 Park Square, Milton Park, Abingdon, Oxon, OX14 4RN
605 Third Avenue, New York, NY 10017

Routledge is an imprint of the Taylor & Francis Group, an informa business

First issued in paperback 2020

Copyright © 2018 Taylor & Francis

Translation by Ken Schubert

The right of Hans Sjögren to be identified as author of this work has been asserted by him in accordance with sections 77 and 78 of the Copyright, Designs and Patents Act 1988.

Library of Congress Cataloging-in-Publication Data
A catalog record for this book has been requested

ISBN: 978-1-138-48914-1 (hbk)
ISBN: 978-0-367-73504-3 (pbk)

Typeset in Sabon
by Apex CoVantage, LLC

Contents

1 Dynasties in the Age of Capitalism

The world abounds with dynasties, many of them in the economic sphere. Familiar names such as Rockefeller, Rothschild, Morgan, Ford, Porsche, Quandt (BMW), Defforet (Carrefour), Agnelli (Fiat), Toyota, Kikkoman, Michelin, Lee (Samsung), Bosch, Heineken, Walton (Wal-Mart), Sainsbury and Tata are to be found among the international financial and industrial dynasties. Some of them have very long histories. For 16 generations, starting in the thirteenth century, the family business of Kikkoman has produced and sold soy sauce, while the French Wendel family has pursued various industrial activities for 13 generations. The Japanese guest house Hoshi Onsen has been run by the descendants of the founder for 46 generations spanning more than 1,300 years, and the family history of the wine maker Château de Gouline goes back more than 1,000 years. Many started as merchant houses, food and wine makers, banks or investment firms. Others accumulated their fortunes through the exploitation of natural resources during the Industrial Revolution, or have their roots in the expanding production of vehicles and consumer goods during the twentieth century. The latest ones have appeared in the wake of the digital revolution.[1]

Many of the family dynasties have attained great influence in society, from their amassing of economic and social power, even political and moral power. By obtaining access to capital with a long-term perspective to provide for succeeding generations, family dynasties provide a balancing force for the short-term perspective of financial markets.[2] On the other hand, the figures on increasing economic inequality in the word raise questions about the appropriateness of allowing a less regulated accumulation of private fortune. Moreover, a world predicated on the ideal of transparency and meritocracy may see dynasties, with sometimes cronyism, murky structures, patrimony and organizational obfuscation, as a threat to democratic values. The phenomenon of family dynasty has indeed a double nature.

The Nordic countries have more dynasties than most others per capita and in GDP terms.[3] A remarkable 15 Nordic family businesses are among the 500 biggest companies in the world. The willingness, often reluctant, of both the political system and labour movement to accept asset accumulation has helped these Nordic businesses survive. The top 1% of Swedes own close to 25% of the country's wealth, as opposed to 16.5% of Spaniards, where dynasties are also abundant. The pattern has held a firm grip on the Nordic countries since the Industrial Revolution and emergence of free enterprise. The trend is particularly pronounced in comparison with the Anglo-Saxon countries—somewhat less so relative to places like Italy and Germany.[4]

This book describes the factors and dynamics behind the ability of Nordic businesses to grow and thrive from one generation to the next in the process of becoming dynasties. Far from being commercial enterprises, they are a venue for power, philanthropy, passion, conflict, freedom and captivity. Like many other dynasties, the Nordic ones are a witch's brew of Machiavelli's Prince, Marx's belief in the potential of the meritocracy and Smith's baker who works to sustain his family—topped by a spoonful of Weber's Protestant Ethic.

The book explores the behaviour and motivations of families without weighing in on whether such businesses represent the most efficient structure for generating profitability and growth. The fact that 90% of Nordic dynasties trace their roots to towns and rural areas has created both distance and dependence in relation to political elites. Besides, history shows many examples of tension between the government and family representatives. The book also examines the ability of families to manage succession and the impact of their beliefs and values on the spirit of entrepreneurship.

Each and every dynasty owes its birth to one or more individuals with the ability to spawn economic benefit by identifying essential unsatisfied needs. A family business may include cousins, in-laws and partners as well. The power of imagining new products and processes that would serve far-flung burgeoning interests and demands was their great incentive. Change was in their blood. They proceeded with incredible stubbornness and flexible savvy to manifest their dreams and satisfy their curiosity. Defiant of old structures and monopolies, they often flew in the face of the logic and unspoken institutions that governed the industries of their day. They challenged the status quo, won others over to their visions, launched new products, introduced unprecedented processes and evolved into charismatic leaders. They wielded the weapons of frugality and caution to weather recession and weak balance sheets so that the next generation could carry the baton farther. Religious and middle-class virtues informed their principles and business culture.

The Lucky Sperm Club

Family businesses—which have existed long before the Industrial Revolution begat the multinationals we are familiar with today—seem to have been the original method of structuring economic activity. They still constitute a species all their own, weaving together personal and commercial interests in a unique way.[5] As crucial as they are to every era, their child mortality rate is suggested to be fairly high. A study in the United States found that 30% outlived their founders, whereas 13% made it to their grandchildren[6] and 3% to the fourth generation. The absolute number of survivors was impressive nonetheless, the largest ones accumulating large private fortunes.

Another study concluded that 20% of the businesses were still around 60 years after their genesis.[7] Comparative research has shown, however, that the life expectancy of ordinary businesses is no better.[8] John Ward and other leading experts focus on the primary activity rather than the holdings of the entire family, as the yardstick of longevity. John Davis, an expert at Harvard Business School on the succession of family businesses, says that the most successful executives understand that personal and commercial interests do not always coincide and learn to deal with the consequences.[9] The challenge is to separate the two spheres and welcome outsiders to the board and management team without compromising the fundamental objectives of the family.

The key to longevity seems to be a belief in dynamic and flexible boundaries for both "family" and "business." Families with rigid assumptions regarding *what a family is* and/or *what business we are in* are less likely to prevail over generations, according to previous research. The element of flexibility enables adaptability to the changing internal and external environment. In turn, this adaptability seems to be crucial for dynasties searching for a long life.[10] Another insight is that people play multiple roles in a large family business. The cast of characters includes managers, board members and family members. While some people play all three roles, others are only owners. To sort out various interests inherent in these roles and relationships help make sense of any issue or decision within a family firm.[11]

Warren Buffet likes to brag that he belongs to the Lucky Sperm Club of major investors. He forgets the importance of the egg and implies that the next generation will be born with a silver spoon in its mouth. No way. Far from all heirs can bear the weight of an illustrious past. A strong brand reflects previous achievements in terms of both personal finances and contributions to the general prosperity. That's why family businesses are so anxious to be reliable while nourishing relationships with the employees, customers, suppliers and community organizations on which they are so dependent. They barter commitment, caution and sacrifice for long-term success. Insolvency is equivalent to loss of face. The process of pulling down the shutters for good at a store or bank may leave deep emotional wounds. The market is unforgiving and the credibility of the family is forfeited. The Damocles sword of asset depletion turns these enterprises into a vulnerable and circumspect species.

Political ground rules and friendly institutions have been the breeding grounds for successful, expansive Nordic family businesses. The dynasties have never been demure about crawling into bed with the powers-that-be. Lobbying and the right contacts have been their open sesame. Ever since the beginning, regulation of the credit market has been based on the needs of corporations and traditional shareholding structures.

Dynasties are famously fond of catchwords and rules of thumb, which constitute a kind of cultural capital to serve as guideposts for everyone associated with the business. Similarly, the values and principles that inform the venture are passed down from generation to generation. Dinners, get-togethers and family council meetings are perfect opportunities for acquainting children with traditions and unwritten laws. Planning for succession starts early in life. Progeny attend elite boarding schools, meet business partners, hear about the latest developments and absorb expectations that they will follow in the footsteps of their elders. Rituals are of the essence. The Wallenbergs have even been known to celebrate the birthdays of their forbears. The role that the family plays in the economy and labour market is a source of pride and self-esteem. But what is good for the goose is not always good for the gander. The welfare of the individual may be sacrificed at the altar of continuity, and suicide has been the final resort for more than one desperate heir to be.

Transparency may be further down on the list of priorities. Important decisions may be made behind closed doors and outsiders may find themselves peeking through the keyhole. Cohesion and continuity have their advantages as well. Passion for the business and its success makes family members more willing to renounce personal interests in poor economic times. If a recession hits, they may waive their salaries in addition to suspending dividend payments. They are the entrepreneurs with a long view of things. Their importance is magnified in eras of the quick buck and short-term profits.

The ancient practice of primogeniture has given way to a world in which a well-educated daughter is just as likely to the scion of the dynasty. Moreover, the natural branching of the family tree, including in-laws, means that each generation offers a wider selection of people who can take over the business. The trend goes hand in hand with the stricter demands for formal education and experience that are inherent to the digital economy. Outsiders who are willing and able to abide by the values and principles of the family can assume professional leadership. To succeed, they must make up for their alien status by taking advantage of their experience and formal qualifications to maximize benefit for the owners.[12] An outsider who is brought in to serve as managing director must be receptive and respectful of the family's preferences at all times instead of simply resting on past laurels.

This is not to say that the most prominent representatives of dynasties are any less likely to be one of their own. History makes it clear that blood is still thicker than water. The comparative lack of experience typical of the younger generation is redressed with time as its understanding of its patrimony matures in preparation for the flame to be passed on once again.

Family businesses are magnets for new impulses. Dynasties are tenacious and a mainstay of most economies. Studies have shown that in addition to their prevalence and power, these dynasties operate under a set of deep moral and spiritual values, and take a long-term view on wealth creation that they sustain independently of the marketplace.[13] Many of such businesses thrive in the largest developing areas of Asia, not to mention the developed countries of Europe and North America. Empirical evidences confirm the long-standing presence of family-controlled business groups in Italy, France, Germany and Spain.[14] Given rapid population growth coupled with the emancipation of women, dynasties with female leaders will start to emerge in India and other parts of Asia, as well as in the diverse and so-called emerging economies in Latin America. Their prospects remain bright.

Successful family businesses have been able to achieve a balance between control and professional leadership. Thus, they have avoided the Buddenbrooks syndrome of continuing with poor leadership; black sheep have been put aside where they could make no trouble. It is a balance between not letting outsiders into the heart of the firm where the family sets the rules and hiring outside managing directors when the situation calls for it. In an open family-controlled firm, outsiders are able to get to the top of the organization based on their combination of qualifications, experience and cultural understanding of its values.

For the next generation, the heritage of ownership can be an emotional burden, since he or she is judged in relation to the past. Later generations will always be compared with the visionary founder. It is almost impossible for heirs to deliver on the same level, viewed from the outside. If the second generation does as effective a job as the founder, the judgement in the public eye will be "not quite as good." If the heir does a much better job, he or she will be viewed as just as good. This sad story reveals the scope and influence of the previous generation and casts a long shadow ahead on subsequent efforts. This faith might explain why succession is a critical phase, associated with conflicts in the family, before, during and afterwards.

The old generation has many chances to prepare. Resources can be devoted to the most talented youngsters, giving them proper educations, international experience and practical learning opportunities. If no one is interested in participating in the operating activities of the business, ownership can remain within the family, including board position, either directly or through an investment company or foundation. In these cases, outsiders are hired to take care of daily operations in each industry.

Mature and Emerging Dynasties

It is characteristic of a dynasty that a family or clan has succeeded in obtaining and maintaining a dominant position in one sector of society.

In the political sphere, there are royal families and princely and ducal houses within which political power has been inherited from one generation to the next. Sometimes the word *dynasty* is used synonymously with an entire period in a nation's history when a king or emperor held political power. The epic novel *Buddenbrooks* by Thomas Mann describes a typical lifecycle of a family business—sometimes referred to as *the Buddenbrooks syndrome*.[15] It consists of three stages or generations: creation, maintenance and decline, or "from rags, to riches to ruins" or "building to consolidating to divesting" or "from shirt sleeves to shirt sleeves in three generations" or "clogs to clogs." The founder builds up his enterprise, often on the basis of a clever innovation; the second generation administers the firm without further innovations; and the third generation concentrates on interests other than those of the founder, including cutting corners, self-indulgent luxurious living, and the fortune is thus dissipated. However, the discontinuity of family businesses is not so much a consequence of internal matters as external conditions. Many dynasties have expired due to various exogenous chocks, such as war, political revolution, financial crisis or the implementation of a less favourable institutional infrastructure.

The Buddenbrooks syndrome has become an engrained, ominous myth that business consultants worldwide use to market their services at times of succession. But the concept of the life-cycle is an old wives' tale that is more prone to arouse fear than confidence (creating business opportunities for consultants eager to sell their services for family members of the second and third generation). It lacks any scientific basis or historical basis, the Nordic dynasties being no exception. A common fallacy is to associate a family with a single core business, given that it and any number of other companies are commonly divested every once in a while for purposes of expansion within the same or other industries. Long-term entrepreneurial viability should be the real yardstick of success.[16] An accurate overview of how well the dynasties with controlling interests in various groups of companies do over the long run requires a focus on the particular families involved.

Considering the superstitions that abound about family businesses, establishing an objective criterion for what constitutes a dynasty is essential. One criterion from which this book proceeds is that the controlling interest last for at least four generations. Even if the interest varies between different core businesses over time, the total holdings are the subject of analysis.

The second criterion is that at least one of the companies achieves the size of a global leader in its industry. The enterprises can represent a number of different sectors as long as the total market value of the holdings is substantial.

The third criterion is that the family be sufficiently influential in the general community that the executive and legislative branches of government are receptive to its views on fundamental economic issues and that the rules of the game by which the private sector plays are amenable to its needs and requirements. Representatives of the family may have conversations with Cabinet members, get involved in official responses to government reports or engage lobbyists to exert pressure on policymakers.

In reality, dynasties come in two stripes—those that have fully blossomed and those that are still budding. Simply stated, the latter type has not maintained a controlling interest for at least four generations although it may meet the other two criteria. By including these dynasties as well, this book is better able to examine whether they exhibit characteristics similar to their mature counterparts. All family firms studied in this book has proven to have a dynastic drive.

However, generally speaking, there are family businesses that have survived for many generations without becoming dynasties. They continue as small- or medium-sized firms and do not become influential in the sense required by the criteria above. As an example, the Swedish family business Berte Qvarn, today associated with SIA Glass, started in 1569, but since its economic impact is limited, it could hardly be categorized as a dynasty. Such family businesses are excluded from this study. We also have cases of dynasties that have disappeared from the scene, after they have proven to be insufficiently competitive. Some of them are mentioned in this book in a counterfactual manner to illustrate mechanisms that are decisive to become a surviving dynasty.

Nordic Dynasties

The book deals with some of the largest family businesses in Denmark, Finland, Norway and Sweden, i.e. the largest Scandinavian or Nordic economies. They represent a variation in terms of age of foundation and industry. For the sake of convenience, all of the firms are referred to as dynasties even though they fall into the two groups discussed earlier: mature and emerging.

In the Danish case, the toy building brick industry Lego and the Kirk Kristiansen family qualify as mature dynasties, as well as the family-controlled shipping company Maersk Group. Danfoss (Clausen family) is world-leading within fluid-control equipment, while Grundfos (Due Jensen family) is the world's largest pump manufacturer and VKR Holding (Kann Rasmussen family) is a pioneer within roof windows. All three firms are run by the third and fourth generation. The study of Danish firms also includes the shoe manufacturer and retailer Ecco Shoes (Toosbuy family), an emerging dynasty run by the second generation.

The Finish dynasties studied are Ahlström, paper and fibre-based materials; G. A. Serlachius, timber and paper; Ehrnrooths, independent industrial and financial firms; Fazer, confectionary and food industry; and

Oras, manufacturer of bathroom and kitchen faucets. The Ahlströms, Ehrnrooths and Fazers are to be recognized as a mature dynasty, while Serlachius has disappeared as an independent firm and Oras is run by the third generation of the Passikivi family.

In the Norwegian case, Andresen, conglomerate; Fred. Olsen & Co, shipping; and Schibsted, media, are living mature dynasties, while the Kiær and Solberg families, timber, made up a dynasty in the early twentieth century but for external reasons lost their industrial role in the 1940s. A survivor is Eidsvold Værk, in the hands of the tenth generation of the family Mathiesen family, although the industrial activities have been sold out.

Among the Swedish ones, the Bonniers, media; the Johnsons, trade and retail; and the Wallenbergs, industrial conglomerate, are fully mature dynasties, while Kamprads, furniture, Ikea; Lundbergs, conglomerate; Olssons, transport; Perssons, retail, H&M; Rausings, packages, Tetra Laval; Stenbecks, conglomerate; and Söderbergs, an investment company, are likely to become mature dynasties. The shipping firms of Broström and Saléninvest could have developed into mature dynasties, but the structural crisis in the 1970s put an end to that, and they are treated marginally in this book.

Missions to Fulfil

The objective is to analyze the evolution of nearly 30 Nordic dynasties. What makes them dynasties and what do they have in common? Obviously, they have created economic value over time, but how has the family unit been used in operation of the business? And how did they overcome difficulties, or not?

The endurance of family businesses is a question of planning for succession and solving conflicts within the family. What is the recipe for smooth succession and the transfer of the jewels of the family crown? And how do families protect themselves from takeovers? How have emerging dynasties prepared themselves to become mature? The challenges might come from the institutional setting. Therefore, to what extent is the survival of the dynasty a result of favourable national polices? The answer to the latter question will be limited to some examples of interdependence between the state and the family.

First, the evolution of Nordic dynasties illustrates the diverse pathways through which large family businesses have faced the challenge of technological change since the first Industrial Revolution. Business life is institutionally determined, even when markets are global. The strategies of Nordic dynasties reflect certain cultural identities. They mirror both the Judaeo-Christian world, bourgeoisie values and the emergence of a welfare model. The Nordic case clearly shows that family businesses are not just products of market imperfections: they start, grow and endure in well-governed and highly industrialized countries. Notably, family businesses are even vital in countries that are reckoned to be among the most secular and individualistic in the world, i.e. the Nordic area.

Second, it is time to revise the view of the family as a backward institution. The controlling family should be viewed as a hub of industrial and business competence, which emphasizes the family as a unit of entrepreneurship and long-term committed leadership. A family starts from an innovative break with industry logic, which gives them a competitive edge close to a monopoly. The business model encapsulates a vision that is attractive for a large organization of both non-family and family members. In the generations to come, whether heirs are willing and qualified to succeed is decisive. Besides, there are numerous examples of family businesses that have not been able to solve conflicts between siblings, cousins and second cousins when ownership has been diluted in later generations. Even if managers are hired for executive positions, ownership and control can stay in the hands of the family. The key is to maintain a distance between family interests and those of the firm, for example by installing a family advisory board or transferring the voting shares to a foundation.

Third, it is time to emphasize the importance of a supportive government for the endurance of dynasties. For society, having families in charge of big business means that people of flesh and blood are at the centre of economic development, to be hold accountable for the actions of the firms. The family could be viewed as a unit that functions as a trustworthy institution in a market economy. From the point of view of the family, the fear of losing trust, reputation and economic value makes it necessary to be "approved by the government" in order to continue accumulating private fortunes, resources and economic power. If welfare society perceives benefits from dynasties in terms of employment, taxes, economic growth and philanthropy, there may be a symbiotic relationship between the government and the families as a keystone in preserving democratic capitalism.

The book starts with a theoretical framework, a review of previous studies and a presentation of a conceptual model, in the chapter "The Theory of Dynasty." The model launches a new set of concepts to study corporate governance of large family businesses, as key factors explaining endurance throughout generations. In the two following chapters, "New Industry Logic" and "Strategy, Structure and Dynamics," the model is applied to the evolution of the Nordic dynasties, i.e. the entrepreneurship and the dynamics in terms of investing, divesting and creating economic value. In the next chapter, "Values and Credos," we look at the rules of the thumb that have inspired, motivated and formed certain types of corporate cultures. Then follows a chapter on succession, "Blood Is Everything—Succession," showing various ways of solving such problems. This chapter also treats the new role of women in this traditionally patriarchal world.

The last empirical chapter, "Business, Politics and Culture," treats the practice of building alliances to the political sphere and branding the family name. It explores how families protect their interests from outsiders, for example by using dual voting shares, box-in-box or setting up a foundation to guarantee the stake in the long run. Besides being active in political debate to change policy as part of the lobbying system, many families engaged in philanthropy and use narratives to communicate values inside and outside the organization. Making use of the family history has a dual meaning: disciplining and unifying the organization and standing out as a trustworthy agent in a market economy. The final chapter, "Conclusion," summarizes the findings and looks at the future of dynasties.

Notes

1. Rose (1995); Colli (2003); James (2006); and Landes (2007).
2. Jaffe and Lane (2004), p. 98.
3. The labels "Nordic" and "Scandinavia" will be used synonomously, although many exclude Finland in "Scandinavia".
4. Own statistical study based on Global Family Business Index, Forbes Global list of the world's 2,000 largest public firms in 2016 and the Fortune Global list of the world's 500 largest firms in 2015.
5. Johannisson (2012).
6. Economist (18 April 2014), p. 14.
7. Ward (2004), p. 5.
8. Wennberg et al. (2011).
9. Economist (1 November 2014).
10. Corbetta and Salvato (2012).
11. Magretta (1998).
12. Hall and Nordqvist (2008).
13. Jaffe and Lane (2004).
14. Colli and Fernández Pérez (2013) and Fernández Pérez and Lluch (2016).
15. Mann (1901).
16. Zellweger et al. (2012).

2   The Theory of Dynasty

An exploration of this subject unearths a network of entrepreneurship, kinship, controlling interests, leadership, political intrigue and economic adventurism. The study of a particular dynasty is interdisciplinary by its very nature, incorporating business management, economic history, ethnology, sociology, etc. The challenge is to identify terms and concepts broad enough to address far-reaching issues, as well as analytical tools with the precision required to draw general conclusions from empirical data. This chapter discusses previous research on the intersection of corporate governance and family businesses, as well as presenting an overview of the journey to mature dynasty. The conceptual model introduced at the end sets the stage for the subsequent empirical chapters.

Personal, Family-Based and Managerial Capitalism

Dynasties frequently exhibit the following patterns. The adventurous spirit of the founder spawns a technological, organizational or market innovation. The idea of establishing a dynasty is remote at best during this stage. The governance structure is ad hoc and implicit, but keep room for a personal vision of trying to get as big as possible. The desire to start a business instead of being employed and serving the interests of others is the primary motive. Gusto, creativity and commitment can be brought to bear in gaining a firm grasp of every angle of the enterprise. Whether a formal corporation or not, the business is still relatively small and totally controlled by the founder.[1]

No responsibilities have been delegated to a management team, which is made up of the same individuals as the board. Small-scale production is the name of the game. The next stage evolves when additional members of the family become involved, as team of siblings or father and daughter. The company may still be unlisted with highly restricted board membership. Just as common, however, is that certain posts go to other people at this point. The strategy is to renew business while the governance structure is built on implicit policies.[2] Production of goods and services accelerates while the organization acquires hierarchical traits as ownership and management begins to assume separate identities.

A strong management team wields essentially all the power in a mature dynasty. The holdings have become so diversified that there are not enough family members to fill all the positions. They focus on the work of the board while professional managers take charge of day-to-day activities. The board involves outsiders and has formal policies concerning corporate governance. They family may hold only minority interests in some of the companies for which other owners and an independent CEO has assumed most responsibility. The dynasty consists of a holding company—a business group—with diversified assets. The family control different branches with the overall strategy to sustain profitability and generate new wealth. Any short-circuit in the information loop can be repaired by an articulate spokesperson who indoctrinates managers and executives in the value of complying with the needs of the family. In the case of a majority interest and exclusive control over the particular individuals who are on the board and management team, the potential to influence corporate governance is automatically greater. Mature dynasties are often a composite of both types of companies, i.e. minority and majority holdings.

A family business is not necessarily a precursor to a full managerial led industrial capitalism. More typically, a mixed breed evolves after the founder has engaged other members of the family. Occasionally a family actually acquires a controlling interest in a large anonymously owned group. Nevertheless, there is generally little lure for companies with conventional management to return to the initial family-oriented arrangement.

Financial and Human Capital

Entrepreneurship is frequently dependent on bank loans, equity capital or other seed financing during the start-up phase. Once the tiller starts to ring, a family owned company has less need of external funding and is often so expansive that it can remain private and snub the stock market. Remaining unlisted also has the advantage of retaining control within the family. Reporting requirements are less, the media are not as likely to be on your back and your transaction costs are reined in. Corporate governance may be a lot soberer when the next quarter's bottom line escapes the glare of the public eye.

Two common defences of the private route are the inability of the market to price in strategic choices and the disadvantage inherent to being dependent on short-sighted owners and financiers who do not share the family's interests. Such a utopia is feasible, however, only if the investment and working capital requirements have been met in another manner. A family that is motivated to enrich itself even if profitability suffers in the process is more likely to avoid the stock market as well. The ideal capital structure minimizes exposure to lenders, shareholders and other third parties, as well as vulnerability to financial crises. The ultimate arrangement is based on the long-term objective of preserving the enterprise within the confines of the family and its interests.

The generations that succeed the founder define the business and articulate a series of empirical principles for corporate governance based on the successes and failures intrinsic to family ownership. During periods of poor profitability or crisis, the family may require the assistance of banks, national or regional foundations, legal experts, relatives, friends and other third parties to ensure ongoing control. At such decisive points, the confidence of the market—maybe even the economic benefits that the business offers as seen through the eyes of cabinet ministers—endures a trial by fire.

Economic booms permit the construction of a financial foundation for additional growth, including human resources. Placing a pool of family members at elite boarding schools and practical degree programs provides a renewable source of knowledge capital. If nobody in the family possesses the requisite skills, high achievers with suitable training are brought in from the outside. They are initiated, try their hand at various positions and assimilate the traditions of the particular culture. The misfortune of having been born elsewhere is offset by sensitivity to the intentions and general assumptions of the family. Ideally they provide a shot in the arm where needed.

A string of successes that stretch across several generations, accompanied not only by profitability but a hospitable political climate, can set the stage for a dynasty. The businesses expand, some of them to established strong global brands. The roles of the family are spelled out and the identity of the business is etched in the mind of the public and the market. The family experiences and communicates its pride in that which the various generations have accomplished in the service of themselves, the nation and the community as a whole. Shares that entitle the holder to different numbers of votes, interlocking ownership, joint board members and other devices can be used to protect a controlling interest. The political establishment and general community follow the business in a way that accrues to the advantage of the family.

Dynastic Longings

The family acquires a more profound grasp of the private sector and its dynamics by virtue of having carried out the practical duties of ownership. The tacit understanding of that which constitutes a successful approach is transmitted to executives of the companies that the family controls. The network traces the circumference of the entire business and the informal contract implies unquestioning loyalty. Owners who perceive a lack of allegiance use various methods of setting things straight. They might not resort to Michael Corleone's tactics, but the goal of eliminating threats to the family's interests can be at least as effective. No dynasty lacks a hierarchy, and the person at the top exercises power in ways that vary from mild indulgence to ostracism.

Meanwhile, caution and deliberation shape the corporate governance of large family owned companies in order to nurture the reputation and renown that they have earned. Not only is the spirit of entrepreneurship, but dynastic longings, now in the driver's seat. Transmission of the family's history becomes integral to the task of maintaining a prominent position in the economic life of the country. Advertising agencies, marketing divisions and journalists produce favourable stories about the family and business for strategic communication with prospective customers and suppliers. Equally typical of a mature dynasty is that some of its profits are siphoned off in the service of foundations. Among the many reasons for doing so are to ensure retention of power in the family, sustain a culture of giving, fund research, evade tax or establish a buffer for poor economic times. Generous donations and strategic storytelling reinforces both the legitimacy of the businesses throughout the community and confidence in the brand among customers. The family devotes its hard-won resources to enumerating the ways that it has promoted national prosperity down through the decades, acted responsibly in the market and taken seriously its role in dealing with the challenges faced by the economy.

This generic overview suggests that the road to dynasty is long and littered by potential dead ends. History is, however, replete with examples of businesses that are founded with dynasty in mind and that eventually expands upon, and realize, the vision due to the tenacity and flexibility of succeeding generations. Let me illustrate this by a statement from the founder of the Wallenberg dynasty. A letter in 1876 from André Oscar Wallenberg to Knut Agathon, his oldest son, may serve as an illustrative example.[3]

> Turning sixty may not be the most cheerful event of my life, but I am comforted by the readiness of your generation to take over. My most heartfelt desire is that my ideas and SEB, my brainchild, live on and that you remember the maxim that maintaining an enterprise is easier than starting over.

He wrote to his 14-year-old son Marcus two years later that he hoped to proceed with his effort to simplify the monetary system "for the sake of humanity." Obviously a heavy responsibility for a young teenager to shoulder. After studying law at Uppsala University, Marcus succeeded in amending the legislation along the lines that his father had advocated in the parliament.

Beyond will and determination, fortunate circumstances—not the least of which are a hospitable political climate, a dynamic economy and regulations that encourage entrepreneurship—are needed if a dynasty is to fully manifest. The Wallenberg fortunes would have fallen by the wayside as early as the financial crisis of 1878–1879 if the government had not extended a helping hand. Financier and industrialist Ivar Kreuger was not so lucky when his hopes for dynasty went up in the flames of the 1929 Wall Street crash. The bête noire of economic booms that ricocheted into financial crises was also the downfall of subsequent dynastic ambitions. And what would have happened if Axel Wenner-Gren, the entrepreneur of the 1930s who identified the potential of the new industrial economy and its technology to satisfy the needs of the average consumer, had left any descendants? Electrolux and his other businesses made him one of the wealthiest people in Sweden for an entire decade. But his contributions to channelling the forces of industrialism and modern life died with him. His empire rose and fell in the matter of one generation.[4]

Churchill's Favourite Marmalade?

Endurance and long-term thinking are typically associated with family businesses that survive the changing of the guard. While such virtues can evoke images of unwieldy structures and obsolete values, they just as often go hand in hand with a strong and effective brand. A name that has lasted since 1670 is a powerful symbol of both excellence and uniqueness. The appeal is to the customer's need of quality, experience, financial stability, family tradition, a winning corporate culture or other trappings of a well-run business. The omnipresence of a long history is accompanied by sentiments with which customers, suppliers and employees can easily identify. The concept of the long haul is embedded in the principles that everyone strives to uphold.

The knowledge that the marmalade in the refrigerator was launched by genial old Mr Pilkington in 1813 and has been a staple of English breakfasts ever since ties us to traditions however arcane, as well as quality in a more visceral sense. Had it been Winston Churchill's favourite, its popularity would have known no end. But the real truth about a brand may be paradoxical, crouching beneath the surface a series of crises during which only wealthy relatives, bailouts from a bank or government intervention saved the country from bankruptcy. Public relations efforts studiously avoid mention of such histories. Brandishing the banner of long-term focus and commitment is a means of demonstrating the commitment of the business to continue serving its customers as promised. Whether such intentions are fully realized is highly uncertain given that nobody knows who or what is lurking around the next corner.

Ants and Grasshoppers

The academic literature on long-lived family businesses, only a fraction of which delves into dynasties, suggests that prudent decisions and low indebtedness are among the important keys to success. Caution is particularly well-advised considering that a lapse in judgement can have devastating social consequences by destroying the family's reputation for business acumen beyond its material wealth. Family businesses have been likened to ants that plod along and evolve organically, as opposed to grasshoppers that engage in acquisitions and mergers to grow faster at the expense of high indebtedness and decentralized ownership. An ant follows the beaten path while a grasshopper may land in dangerous unchartered territory.[5]

Some historical research has explored ways that the family as an entity is exploited to overcome various types of obstacles. Frugal use of available resources and the opportunity for continual learning are two such strategies. Similarly, training of the younger generation at schools and businesses abroad paves the way for establishing a foothold in new, profitable international markets. Transcending barriers and completing projects with credibility intact frequently requires stationing members of the family in different parts of the world for a period of time. Studies have found that the family may be well positioned to mobilize the resources that the company needs to confront new challenges and maintain the vitality of its business relationships. Transaction costs decline by virtue of the regional, ethnic and religious bonds that are inherent to kinship and that generate their own particular types of synergies. A business rooted in deep-seated family traditions can also extend the sense of intimacy to other employees in a way that sets the stage for a stronger international presence.[6]

Research findings suggest that knowledge and expertise acquired and shared by owners and managers are often unique. Once two or three generations have passed, a company that replaces its managing director and majority owner every five years will have trouble preserving the family's repository of knowledge about customers, markets and suppliers. The passion for product and entrepreneurship evolve to a deep-seated commitment that infuses the brand and identity of the company itself. The long view spills over into a sense of affinity with suppliers, customers, regional growth and the environment. Research has made it clear that local ownership with a human countenance is a boon to the community.[7]

The other side of this rosy picture is the tendency of dynasties to seize considerable power in the market, establishing fiefdoms and cartels that exclude new entrepreneurs eager to join the fray. And the wealth they accumulate over time widens socioeconomic gaps, particular when growth is low and returns are high. Employment income during such periods is subservient to the profit generation capacity of fortunes large and small. Economic historians have estimated that capitalists need reinvest but one-fifth of their annual return to ensure long-term asset growth. While the wealth created by dynasties aggravates economic inequality even more as a result, the impact is less if foundations rather than private managers handle the money.[8] Nevertheless, the increasing economic inequality in the world raises key questions, for the representatives of family dynasties to tackle, as what are the purpose of the generated wealth, what should we achieve for it, and how should it be re-distributed to the society in large?

Dynasties may also hobble democracy by forming economic and political alliances that raise costs for consumers, hinder entrepreneurs and stymie the growth of profitable businesses. The purpose of political liaisons is to enjoy tax and other advantages that provide a competitive edge in the market. Another source of criticism is the view that dynasties are bastions of male supremacy, secret networks and smoke-filled rooms that promote nepotism and other forms of corruption. A world predicated on the ideal of transparency may see dynasties, with their murky structures and organizational obfuscation, as a threat to democratic values.[9]

Their very fabric reflects the institutions and cultures of the countries in which they do business. If tax rates are high, a company benefits from investing its holdings and earnings elsewhere by means of fancy legal and organizational footwork. The lack of transparency has other causes in developing countries with their corrupt and unwieldy ruling elites.

Since the rise of large American corporations after World War II, dynasties in the industrial world have evolved while ownership and management glide apart. The challenge for family run businesses has been to water the soil for ongoing investment and innovation while continuing to hold a majority interest. A number of them have fallen short of the mark and had to surrender power to independent management along with public and private ownership. The many who have risen to the challenge frequently acquire venture capital to keep pace with the competition and the forces of globalization.

Steadfast financiers have been crucial to their success. Research has shown that dynasties emerge at the crossroads of ground-breaking innovation and entrepreneurial leadership. Only the most patient financiers can withstand the risk, uncertainty and delayed return associated with investment in modernization and new technology. Adopting a long-term view and being willing to accept year after year of losses in the service of a promising product are vital during recessions and financial crises. The innovation process also demands support from other stakeholders who are thoroughly versed in the industry. Companies under stalwart leadership are better positioned to stave off internal conflicts of interest and organizational rigidity. Thus, dynasties tend to own innovative companies that are able to see the big picture. Many leading dynasties possess the kind of highly sophisticated knowledge about their industries that allows them to manage and grow their holdings over long periods of time.[10]

The Good Life Outside the Stock Market

Today's dynasties began on a small scale: wooden toys that became Lego and a world-leading industry; experiments in a boyhood attic that develop into a world leading firm within fluid control equipment (Danfoss); or a new type of container for liquids (tetrahedrons, Tetra Pak), or Windsor (spindle) chairs that could be placed in a package and left on a milking stool (Ikea). Individuals have challenged previously existing products or procedures with creative thinking and entrepreneurship. They have formed a new industry logic. An idea has been transformed into a proto- type, which has turned into an innovation with large-scale production. In its earliest phases, entrepreneurial activity has required access to outside capital, such as a bank loan, venture capital or some other source of seed capital. Once profits started to accumulate, the family business's need for financiers declined substantially. It is worth noting that many companies belonging to dynasties are unlisted: they simply had no need for the stock market in order to expand. Being listed, moreover, is associated with sub- stantial costs. In addition, being constantly in the spotlight of the market and media increases transactions costs.

It is likely that avoiding the public scrutiny associated with quarterly report capitalism permits operational flexibility and practices that would not otherwise be possible. Common arguments of controlling owners of unlisted firms are that the market is incapable of evaluating long-term strategies and that it is beneficial not to be dependent on (short-sighted) owners and financiers who do not share the family's goals. Another motive for staying away from the stock exchange is that it might make it possible for the family, as controlling owners, to act in their own interest, even at the expense of the firm.

Mature Nordic dynasties trace their roots back to the Industrial Revo- lution of the late nineteenth century, while the younger ones were born after World War II. The founder in each case was the citizen of a Nor- dic country and registered the business there. Both the majority interest and the family fortune may, however, have been abroad. Some dynasties do not list their core holdings, or even the business itself, on a stock exchange. The company has reinvested its earnings for organic growth without the financial assistance of banks or the stock market. Quarterly reports and short-term forecasts are only millstones around the neck of owners who are out to minimize transaction costs and maximize long- term profitability. Visibility on the stock market is also a fast way to attract those who would like nothing better than to obtain a board post and influence the direction of the company.

Ownership is often directly tied to great wealth. Ingvar Kamprad (Ikea) and Stefan Persson (H&M) have been on the list of the 20 wealthiest people in the world over the past 10 years, while second and generation Rausings have long been among the most affluent families in the UK. The Kristiansens, who own Lego (unlisted), Mærsk Mc-Kinney and Kann Rasmussen have been at the top of the heap in Denmark.

A Conceptual Model

It has been argued that family firms do not require a special theory on their own since they behave as non-family firms (it is necessary to identify something distinctive in order to justify the need for a theory). The only distinctive factor identified among many family firms is the dynastic motive, which makes many them unique and theoretically interesting, and qualifies them for a special theory.[11] Such a theory has to consider the challenge facing family dynasty: to create a governance structure that properly represents all the need of family owners and effectively delegates management to various entities controlled and governed by the family. I will launch five concepts to be applied to the life of family dynasties: long-term committed ownership, network capacity, relational capital, value creation and historical roots.[12]

A general assumption concerning a prosperous society with a rapid rate of innovation and a high level of employment is that private owners—controlling owners—who actively reformulate economic activity and thus guarantee constant (industrial) renewal are required. History has demonstrated that the most common types of such control owners are individuals or families that exercise long-term committed ownership in firms.[13] To be a committed owner requires an ownership interest amounting to at least 5% of the share votes or a role as the firm's principal provider of credit, as well as a seat on the board and the ability to follow and help direct the functions of the firm closely. The latter refers to participation in decisions that concern the company's long-term direction, changes in high-level personnel, and sometimes direct leadership. It should be noted that establishing exact boundaries for these activities involves considerable difficulty.

For a holding to be labelled long-term, it must have passed through at least two downturns, i.e., have remained stable during two periods of weak demand and low profitability. In view of the varying lengths of downturns, both generally and in particular businesses, ownership should not be less than a decade to be considered long-term. This implies that one or more individuals representing the ownership interest served on the board during the period in question.

Both requirements concerning the length and the extent of long-term ownership seem modest in the case of dynasties, as they often involve wholly owned companies and core holdings that stretch over several generations. If stricter requirements are used, however, families that have minority positions in large multinational firms and/or follow strategies that involve the buying and selling of firms would be excluded. Moreover, the qualitative aspects may well be more important. In other words, what is the true goal of the active long-term ownership control that is often concentrated in a majority-owned investment or holding company or a family foundation? It makes sense to take the view that *long-term committed ownership* in the case of dynasties implies that the family assumes responsibility for business renewal and restructuring while stable ownership provides job security and the financial backing necessary to undertake investments that can be profitable only in the long-run. This definition fits well as an overarching concept of long-term ownership as practiced by successful dynasties.

Another characteristic common to dynasties is that they possess *networking capacity*. This means the ability to create, as well as to renew and widen, the relationship of trust with other individuals or groups. The level of network capacity guides the controlling owner in his or her choices with regard to human capital, personal competence and information. Access to a relationships-based network of high quality makes it easier for the owner to achieve his or her pre-established economic goals. Moreover, the social network facilitates the ability to take quick advantage of opportunities as they arise. The effective utilization of networking capacity reduces the costs associated with creating trust in business transactions as well as the ability to keep, renew and expand the available stock of competence within the controlled company. It also increases the ability to encourage individuals, political parties, interest organizations and enterprises outside the family's sphere to take an interest in the future of the companies. High networking capacity is thus a prerequisite for a living dynasty.

Relational Capital and Value Creation

Relational capital is central to the network economy. The concept pinpoints the advantages that individuals create when collaborating on ecoomic activities. The idea is that people can work together to create value that goes beyond the virtues of social intercourse. The fundamental assumption is that relationships are crucibles in which trust and scope for transactions and commercial exchange are forged. The more relational capital, the less uncertainty and the likelier that fraud and other dishonesty will come to light. Traditional market pricing considers only items that can be quantified for use in a cost and income analysis. As a result, relational capital is not a variable in market models. Nevertheless, some of it is needed if companies are to do business with each other on an ongoing basis. Whether relational capital can be quantified and priced is a subject for future research.

With respect to dynasties, it is intimately connected with preparing the up-and-coming generation to carry on the tradition. Strategy and other vital aspects of the enterprise are passed down primarily through discussions around the dinner table, often with the participation of business partners and acquaintances. Holidays, large family get-togethers and various celebrations also cement the bonds between representatives of the past and future. Such gatherings allow people to share ideas and reinforce emotional ties that propagate existing alliances and orient recently acquired inlaws.[14]

Let's talk a little about the concept of *values and principles*. Organizations often spawn a potpourri of slogans, taboos, dictates and rules of conduct that serve as guidelines for employees. The most elementary kind are exhortations to think and act in a particular way. Typically the fruit of bitter experience, they are warning signs of hazards ahead. If the business has experienced a serious crisis, the admonitions may be in no uncertain terms and make it clear that employees have no choice but to obey if they value their jobs. Such informal in-house rules range from light-hearted, perhaps exaggerated or fabricated anecdotes, to fervid commandments intended to impose discipline and an unwavering sense of responsibility, perhaps with a penalty to pay for noncompliance.

Corporate governance is greatly dependent on unwritten rules in the case of dynasties. The purpose of these rules of the game, or informal institutions, is always the same—higher profits and market value. The main representatives of the family frequently include dictates in their wills or otherwise communicate key priorities for the future to employees and the next generation. These acquired insights and understandings constitute a corpus of values and principles, with spill over effects to other stakeholders of the firm, including customers and state authorities. Which is not to say that they always benefit the business. Sometimes they promote inertia and poor strategic choices.

Historical Anchor

The founding of a family business is accompanied by the establishment of a direct line (what I like to call an "historical anchor") between the individual members, management, the boardroom and the political sphere. The line works in three ways—it ensures authority, stability and predictability while limiting the manoeuvrability of outsiders, and legitimatize the business operations in the eye of society. Management and employees are assigned specific roles that are part of the corporate culture and reflect the family's interests. The result is a consensus regarding the questions that need to be addressed, if not the particular answers that are arrived at.

Based on such longstanding mechanisms, an historical anchor is relatively oblivious to the laws and directions of the powers-that-be and regulatory authorities, but shapes the destiny of the organization in conjunction with corporate governance as a whole. Recalibrating the system, which directly influences both long and short-term strategy, would occasion considerable expenses. With the exception of minor institutional adjustments that enable necessary flexibility, investments in the business are generally intended to maintain the status quo. The historical anchor will sustain.

Social scientists may argue that organizations typically achieve cost-effective, long-term technological solutions as the result of happenstance along the way, in the literature conceptually labelled as path dependency. Furthermore, maintaining stability by adapting to the political and legal system is a well-researched concept. Nevertheless, dynasties are a special case that demands particular attention. Both social science observationsassume a choice between various conceivable paths, an equilibrium of sorts. Because dynasties are tied to an historical anchor and do not face competing institutional alternatives, on the other hand, a role for coincidence is inherently ruled out. Moreover, institutional inertia or flexibility is always the result of organization-specific factors. Fundamental to the dynastic structure is that behaviour and identity flows from staging and reconstructing social roles that can evolve over time. Tradition and the personal links to the boardroom establish the parameters for interpretation and enactment of the roles.

Notes

1. Colli (2016).
2. Jaffe and Lane (2004), p. 84.
3. Nilsson (2001), p. 430. See also Lindgren (2011).
4. Glete (1994), pp. 173–6.
5. Miller and Le Breton-Miller (2005). See also Casillas, Acedo and Moreno (2007).
6. Lubinski et al. (2016).
7. Nordqvist (2016).
8. Piketty (2015), pp. 370–3.
9. Morck (2005).
10. Sjögren (2012).
11. Casson (1999).
12. For a more detailed discussion of these concepts, see Carlsson (2007); Sjögren (2012), pp. 14–16; Sjögren (2007), pp. 7–22; Sjögren (2013) and Sjögren (2015), pp. 58–60. For additional studies of long-term committed ownership, social capital and networks, see Glete (1994); Håkansson and Johanson (2001); Arregle et al. (2007); Brundin et al. (2008); Pearson et al. (2008); Lumpkin et al. (2010) and Lindgren (2012).
13. Sjögren (2012).
14. Karlsson Stider (2000), pp. 154–6.

3   New Industry Logic

In the mid-nineteenth century, the Nordic economics were backward in relation to England and other more industrialized countries, Norway and Finland more so than Denmark and Sweden. The incentive for many of the businesses was to catch up in term of economic growth: the Nordic countries were relatively backward in Gerschenkronian terms. All four countries had goods to offer the rest of Europe and soon became large exporters of products within fishery, forestry and mining. In order to carry out this trade, they had to modernize and develop other parts of the economy, for example the infrastructure and financial system. The first generations of the dynasties took part in the formation of a liberalized economy, where they push for institutions that promoted more freedom for business activity. Thanks to natural resources and the dissemination of knowledge and technology, some impoverished economies on the periphery of Europe soon became sophisticated and wealthy, at the beginning of the twentieth century.[1]

Nordic dynasties started off small scale—a new type of carton for liquids (tetrahedron, Tetra Pak), a collapsible milking stool (Ikea), plastic blocks for educational play (Lego). From a prototype, the innovation ultimately morphs into large-scale production. In every case, individuals challenge old solutions by means of vigorous entrepreneurship and creative approaches. They violate the industry's current belief system and create a brand-new market or breathe fresh life into an existing one. The original ideas, innovations and worldviews (historical anchor) always flow in the veins of future generations.

Nordic Dynastic Entrepreneurship in the Nineteenth Century

Many of the original extant dynasties centred on unique Nordic resources while borrowing technologies engendered by the Industrial Revolution. Similarly, their American counterparts were the offspring of oil strikes, steam power, modern banking and expanding foreign trade.

The Danish shipping company A.P. Møller-Mærsk was founded in opposition to the traditional view at the time. Captain Peter Mærsk Møller, an offspring of a family of seamen, was convinced that sailing-ships should be replaced by steamships. Thanks to their construction, steamships were faster and more reliable than sailing ships because they could be scheduled on routes with higher precision than sailing ships, which were dependent on the wind. Their steadiness also meant that fewer goods were damaged during transport. Møller-Mærsk argued that it was also time for smaller harbours to switch to steamships and feared that his hometown of Svendborg in south Fyn would lose more ground to Copenhagen as the major port if it did not. He started a ruckus with representatives of the wooden-built ships in Svendborg after having declared his views in the local newspaper in February, 1899. He received strong criticism from the local community and the newspaper published contributions for six months.[2]

Peter Mærsk Møller had experience of navigating a steamship internationally when he settled down as a senior citizen, and he was convinced that the future belonged to these new ships. In his vision, Svendborg should also host a shipyard of steamships. While the local business community reacted negatively to his plans, he got all the support he needed from his son A.P. Møller. Father and son started to approach people who might like to invest in their joint-stock company, practically door-to-door throughout the village, eager to have an independent company in the hands of their family. Finally, they got enough subscribers of shares, including a local bank, but two-thirds of the share capital of DK 150 000 had to be guaranteed by them. In 1904, A/S Dampskibsselskabet Svendborg was founded and later that year a two-year-old English steamship was bought.[3]

Steam engines belonged to the first Industrial Revolution and were introduced by most industries. In the sawmill industry, they were replacing the hydro power in Finland, where the share of production from water powered sawmills went down from 80% to less than 15% between 1871 and 1896. This transformation was even more marked in the case of Ahlström, where the steam saw totally dominated the business, compared to 20 years earlier, when all sawn goods came from hydro powered sawmills.[4] Antti Ahlström, the founder, was a jack-of-all-trades, combining sawmills with farming, ironworks, trading grains and shipping of sawn goods and paper. For the latter, he used both his own and chartered ships.[5] By 1890s, Antti Ahlström had one of the largest shipping fleets in Finland, and his boats sailed to the Baltic countries, the Mediterranean and as far as Burma and Singapore. Thanks to inheritances, entrepreneurial spirit and commercial interest, he became the largest owner of ironworks and sawmills in Finland. The reason for the expansion was his new way of exploiting timber, used as charcoal for the production of iron.

Ahlström realized the value of forests in terms of raw material and started to build sawmills. Although the business cycles were erratic in the late nineteenth century, the underlying trend was strong international demand for sawed products, where the Finnish estates had much to offer. The book value of sawmills in Ahlström increased seven times between 1888 and 1891 alone, while their share of capital went from 12% to 40%, leaving the ironworks behind.[6] He made a lot of money by converting non-profitable ironworks into sawmills, and by 1900 Ahlström had the largest sawmills in all of Scandinavia.[7] By starting a paper mill in 1907 and a pulp mill in 1917, Ahlström strengthened its position within the wood-processing cluster.[8] When the founder died, his son Walter Ahlström expanded the business group by acquiring two large industrial companies, Warkaus and Karhula. The success of the family was the result of efficient strategies during the industrial breakthrough in Finland.

After the Napoleonic War, a formative period started in Norway, with the constitution of 1814 as an institutional backbone for the business system. The founders of dynasties took part in the movement, both politically and commercially. They invested in trade, shipping, craftsmanship, sawmills, forests and estates, and established new types of financing. Many of the founders were born outside Norway or travelled abroad extensively to acquire international experience.

Several generations of the Mathiesen family in the eighteenth and nineteenth centuries were timber merchants—they acquired extensive tracts of Norwegian forestland. The Mathiesens and Tolstrups shared production at Eidsvold Værk from 1842 until Haaken C. Mathiesen became the sole owner in 1893. The Industrial Revolution played a key role, given that timber from the sawmills could be shipped on a larger scale the more steamboats were available at harbours to carry it to the rest of Europe. After Moelven Brug purchased the manufacturing business in 1994, the Mathiesens turned primarily to forestry and land ownership.[9]

Another Norwegian, Nicolai Andresen, built up a business model based on Danish and German traditions and became the first of six generation, so far, of a dynasty. Through migration and marriages across borders, there was kinship to the other bourgeois families in Europe, which fostered new trade routes. The network to the bourgeoisie in Hamburg was especially important for merchant families. The establishment of the business system was part of a process of nation building, and Andresen argued successfully in the Parliament for the foundation of the first national bank (Norges Bank in 1816; central banking function in 1823), a stock exchange (Christiania Børs in 1819) and a system of savings banks (1822). Designing a supportive financial system, with monetary policy, blanco credits and exchange notes, was necessary in order to break with industry logic. Together with three of his sons, he continued to build the institutional infrastructure within the liberalized merchant economy and paved the way for a family banking house, insurance companies and trading houses. In 1849, his son Johan Henrik bought Tiedemanns Tobaksfabrik, which turns out to be the only branch in the portfolio that survived the third generation of the family business after the difficult times of the early 1920s. Besides, there was a banking company: N. A. Andresen & Co.[10]

The Norwegian industrial breakthrough also hosted stars that flickered out, due to exogenous chocks to the liberalized economy. The family of Kiær and Solberg set up a forest company that expanded to thousands of acres in Finland, Sweden, Russia and Norway, to a book value corresponding to 1% of Norwegian GDP in 1918. The disruption in the interwar years was a result of a combination of external factors, such as the Russian Revolution and the nationalization of foreign firms, the breakup of the gold standard and the Great Depression. The family had built a plant for wood processing and production of paper in Dubrowka, Russia, vertically integrated to supply a large market. When the Soviet government confiscated the plant, the large investments turned into a giant loss, leaving the family with substantial loans that become an even heavier burden because of the deflation of the early 1920s. Gradually, the family business fell into the hands of their creditors, both internationally and at home.[11]

Peter Collett Solberg tried to compensate for the losses by speculating in the market for foreign exchange, but the losses he suffered were even larger than the loss from the debacle in Dubrowka. Monetary policy in the interwar period worked to the disadvantage of most industrial capitalists, and Kiær and Solberg had no bank to rely on for short-term credit (in contrast to the Wallenberg family in Sweden, for example). Since the operations and the contracts were tied to an arrangement of fixed exchange rates, the breakdown of the Gold Standard became overwhelming for this family business. After struggling with financial distress for decades, the third generation of the family gave up and sold the business in 1961, as a tiny residue of the glorious days of grand bourgeoisie in the Norwegian forest industry.[12]

Merchant Houses

The appearance of a Scandinavian bourgeoisie went hand in hand with the establishment of merchant houses, some of which started in partnership with immigrants from Germany, The Netherlands and Great Britain. Over the years, the houses became highly diversified, with export of iron, timber, wood, pulp, grains and import of manufactured and colonial goods.[13] They built large fleets that enabled them to carry out both national and international transport, but they also integrated back and became owners of industrial firms. A main feature was the attempt by the founder to carve out an international profile by learning foreign languages, going on long journeys and widening his network of relationships, i.e., building trust in order to maintain agents and trade all over the world. The new-born interest in North and South America, and a long wave of emigration spurred their entrepreneurship. Many of them set up lines for passenger traffic and trade over the Atlantic. The trade with Russia and some Asian countries was important financially. The combination of international orientation and networking capacity turned out to be an effective strategy for many Nordic shipping firms and merchant houses.

On the east coast of Sweden, the dynasty of the Johnsons has all the attributes of a successful trading and merchant house, while the Broström family is the best example from the west coast, not to say that they divided the trade between them geographically in an oligopolistic way. Both came from regions where many people emigrated to the United States because of poverty and bad soil. As "immigrants" in Gothenburg and Stockholm, they stick to the ideal of being independent of creditors and other investors when setting up their own business.

In 1865, founder Axel Broström purchased the galleon "Mathilda" and started freight transport between his hometown of Kristinehamn and Gothenburg. Twenty-five years later, he established what was to become the parent company of the Broström Group, Ångfartygs AB Tirfing, located in central Gothenburg, where the family had settled down. His son Dan Broström was talented within shipping and gained a leading role in the company, establishing the Swedish American Line in 1915. Over the years, Broström expanded into various companies, as the liner companies Swedish Orient Line and Swedish East Asiatic Company and the shipyard Eriksberg. Until the crisis in the shipyard industry of the 1970s, Broströms was at the top of the Swedish shipping industry.[14]

The other Swedish example was the Johnson family. In 1873, a 29-year-old son of a saddler from Jönköping started a trading business in Stockholm, A. Johnson & Co. The basis was the export of iron and the import of coal. The coal business led to shipping in 1890 (Rederiaktiebolaget Nordstjernan), while the iron business eventually led to a majority holding in an ironworks in 1905 (Avesta Jernverk). When the founder died, his 35-year-old son Axel inherited a substantial fortune, a trading house, a shipping line and an ironworks. He established the world's first fully diesel-powered ocean-going fleet and the first oil refinery in Scandinavia. After his death in 1958, his oldest son became the head of some 100 companies with more than 22,000 employees.[15]

Generally speaking, the repeal of the Navigation Act in 1849 brought favourable times to international trade and shipping. In Norway, Fred. Olsen saw the same opportunity to expand on the seven seas as Møller in Denmark and Broström and Johnson in Sweden. The Norwegian family business started in 1848 in a small village on the Oslo Fjord, Hvitsten, when three brothers of the Olsen family became sea captains at an early age. The business took off when Thomas Fredrik (Fred.) Olsen, the son of the middle brother, created a network of regular liner services, first on the North Sea and later for remote destinations. He built up a reputation of trustworthy service and realized the necessity to shift from sail to steam in order to increase dependability. In 1897, Fred. Olsen ordered his first steamship and before World War I he had invested in an even better technology: motor ships. The office moved from Hvitsten to Oslo, where he continued to open new international lines, including to South America, Baltic ports and the west coast of the Unite States through the Panama Canal. Viewed as a dynamic and competent leader with a high level of networking capacity, Fred. Olsen was frequently asked to take over the management of Norwegian lines in trouble.[16]

Even before World War I, the family business of Fred. Olsen came to play a dominant role in international trade from Norway to ports around the world. After the war, when 23 out of 44 ships had been destroyed, the fleet was rebuilt and in 1929 Fred. Olsen & Co acquired its first tanker and started to construct a modern fleet of fast freight services for the Mediterranean and Canary routes. The control of ownership was transferred to the third generation from the founder, to the sons Rudolf and Thomas, who had been partners in the firm since 1914 and 1922 respectively. They took the initiative to start an aircraft manufacturer in Norway, DNL, which contributed to the birth of the Scandinavian Airline System (SAS) in 1946.[17]

Because all these businesses were heavily reliant on the new technology of steam power, their break with old assumptions and ways of doing things was hardly unique or sufficient to explain their success. They did, however, manage to monopolize their national markets at a time when competition was much less daunting than it is these days. As a result, they could exploit European demand for exports of Nordic raw materials, refined or otherwise. The hefty profits they generated in a relatively period of time lent them extraordinary vitality. As was typical of the entrepreneurial business climate that arose during the transition from the agricultural to industrial economy, all the fortunes were amassed outside the big cities. Ownership and decision-making was in the hands of the founder since such profit-generating businesses had very limited dependence on bank loans. The personal nature of the start-up phase evolved to a collective effort only after production became large scale and more family members were involved.

Sometimes the expansion did not involve much of a rupture with industry tradition. Per Olof Söderberg, the son of a merchant, started a business in the early 1860s to sell Bessemer steel in the Swedish market from Stockholm. The product came from the new Högbo steelworks, the initial sprout of what was to become the Sandvik group. Söderberg & Haak grew into a wholesale business for iron and steel. Olof Söderberg of the next generation carved out a prominent position for the company in Stockholm, including holdings in multiple new manufacturers. Representatives of the third generation consolidated the family's interests in an investment company that boasted of diversified ownership and was listed in 1947. The family maintained its control by means of direct ownership and a couple of new foundations, bonding with the Wallenbergs by serving together on the boards of countless Swedish manufacturers, particularly in Bergslagen.[18]

Johan, Erik and Sven Söderberg marched ahead when the time for the fourth generation rolled around. Despite their dedication to family and the business, the Söderberg dynasty did not shake up the industry in the sense of having a significant impact on economic transformation. Their contributions never went beyond managing equity portfolios and investing in sure winners. Nevertheless, their dogged board efforts helped shore up and stabilize a whole series of successful businesses that had emerged from the Industrial Revolution. Ratos was formed largely to solve the problems associated with the business of a growing family by obtaining a market valuation of equity transactions. Based on prudent investment policies and expanding portfolios, the foundations have become key sources of grants for education and research.

Banking and the Bourgeoisie

The industrial revolution in Scandinavia was a breakthrough for a new type of bank lending, progressive enough to support the gushing industries. The first modern bank in Sweden was founded in 1855, when André Oscar Wallenberg launched a new banking program on the northeast cost of Sweden, a district where sawmills flourished. These innovations were used in the Filialbanken Sundsvall with its services actively marketed in the local process. The marketing was an innovation in itself, since lending institutions had traditionally been "silent" organizations.[19] On the basis of the experience, Wallenberg founded a bank in the capital of Sweden in 1856, Stockholms Enskilda Bank, which soon became a trendsetter in operational terms. Though this was an ordinary bank chartered with the privilege of note issue—joint stock banks came 10 years later—it managed to attract a large percentage of the deposit market in Stockholm by introducing new instruments of deposit. For the first time, the operations of a Swedish bank were largely based on stockholders' equity and deposits by the public.

Moreover, the new bank introduced new ways of managing real and efficient payment transfers within the economy. The regional *enskilda* banks were allowed to open free-of-charge transfer accounts at Stockholms Enskilda Bank. Subsequently, a network of commercial banks was built up to bring distant regions together into a national system for clearing and paying. That facilitated the transfer of capital from regions with a surplus to those with a deficit. As of the 1860s, extensive branch banking further stimulated this process of integration of financial capital. Financial intermediation and various systems for transferring payments and credits were a natural development due to an immature financial infrastructure and the need for transactions in a growing economy. The determined effort by Wallenberg broke with industry logic in banking, which was necessary for this industrial breakthrough to occur in the relatively backward economy of Sweden.[20]

The Industrial Revolution gave birth to a new class—the bourgeoisie. They were agents in the liberalization of society and started many new commercial activities, not least by lobbying and representation in the parliament. When the education system was democratized with six years of compulsory schooling in 1842, the literacy rate started to increase.[21] This made the public capable of developing, absorbing and discussing new ideas. Thanks to typography, agents could make use of low entry costs to start printing houses and newspapers, which were affordable for the great masses of people. In this tradition, Gerhard Bonnier started a lending library in Copenhagen in 1804, and soon after a publishing house. Three of his sons emigrated to Sweden where they established themselves within publishing, including the start of a newspaper in Gothenburg in 1859. Thanks to their skills and networking capacity, they soon dominated the production of fiction for adults and children. In 1900, they acquired a stake in of the largest morning newspaper in Stockholm, *Dagens Nyheter*, but they also developed the market for magazines.[22]

The Norwegian Schibsted Group also started by printing books in Christiania (later Oslo) in 1839. As of 1843, Christian Schibsted was the sole owner. The investment in a new printing machine made it possible to start a newspaper—*Aftenposten*. There were already newspapers in the market, but Schibsted introduced a broad public paper cheaper and with a more decent style then the main competitor, a newspaper that had been disparaged by politicians and consumers. Christian Schibsted took control of the editorial content and hired less provocative editors. Thanks to the competitive price, he took advantage of the increasing demand for simple news and small adverts: during urbanization, people from the countryside could not afford the more expensive alternatives. Coming from a peasant family in poverty, put in a bridewell as a nine-year old kid, Schibsted was aware of the conditions of the working class.[23] As a newcomer to the city bourgeoisie, he understand the demand for a paper that mirrored ordinary life in an objective way, which he formulated as follows: "keep prices low, enabling more and more people from have-not classes to purchase a newspaper . . . with a promise that the paper will be written in a human and well-behaved style."[24]

In Finland, many family businesses started in the forest industry. In the firms of both Ahlström and G. A. Serlachius, timber was exported to western countries, although Russia was the largest single market. Denmark took advantage of steam engines to develop their trade and shipping, with Mærsk Møller as an interesting example. Merchant capitalism and the formation of a new business system also characterized Norway and Sweden, particularly the families of Andresen, Broström and Johnson. Many of the emerging dynasties were inspired by ideologists, bankers and industrialists in the UK and Germany; ideas and technology were transferred and further developed, not least by publishers like the Bonniers and Schibsteds. The increasing demand for timber, sawn products, fish and iron ore abroad was met by a supply of vast natural resources, especially in Finland, Norway and Sweden. As a result, the Nordic economies established downstream relations to a network-based European economy and upstream relations to peasants, workers and entrepreneurs.

In this transformation of the economy, the bourgeoisie emerged as a distinguished group of capitalists. They were all critical for the transformation to an industrial society. The families of Ahlström, Andresen, Kiær and Solberg, Mathiesen and Wallenberg soon became influential, both economically and politically. Their entrepreneurial spirit and operations broke with business models in the Nordic countries. They used all available resources to close the gap to the forerunners among the European countries in the quest for domestic economic wealth.

Urbanization and the rise of civil society paved the way for new market segments for various consumer products and durable goods. The bourgeois culture in the cities nurtured an interest in treats like pastries and chocolate. In the case of Fazer, breaking with industry logic meant starting factories to manufacture candy in Helsinki. At that time, most confectionery products were imported from Russia, and Karl Fazer noticed the strong demand for sweets in Finland. However, the choice of career was not that obvious. His parents had emigrated from Switzerland and started a fur business in their new homeland, satisfying the demand for warm clothes among Finns. As a youngster, Karl fell in love with the Finnish countryside, spent time wandering in the woods and thought of becoming a forester. However, since his weaknesses for taste was even stronger, he decided to be a confectioner against his father's wishes and spent two years as a journeyman in St. Petersburg to study the famous French-Russian confectionery industry. After an additional year as employee at two Russian firms, he worked in Berlin and Paris before starting his own business back in Finland at the age of 24: a French-Russian confectionery café at the best location in Helsinki. Not surprisingly, it was not his father that guaranteed the first loan, but one of the richest businessmen in Helsinki, K.H. Renlund, who had also started with "two empty pockets" and a strong entrepreneurial spirit.[25]

There were already confectionery cafés and another "factory" established in Helsinki at the time when Karl Fazer started his business. However, his business model was more attractive: he spoiled the citizens with coffee, chocolate, pastry and cookies of high quality at fair prices. The location was optimal, in the middle of the commercial area close to the university. On the manufacturing side, the only competitor produced cheap, simple and handmade candy and was outrivaled when Karl Fazer decided to start manufacturing on a large-scale basis at a new four-storey factory in 1898. Until then, imported sweets from Russia had been duty-free, but a new regulation introduced a significant import duty. This opened the door to large-scale domestic production and Fazer was eager to take advantage of demand. The institutional change turned out to have a substantial impact and the import of sweets from Russia had almost disappeared after three years. The first country to import was England, starting in 1898. The brand received an extra boost after Fazer awarded prizes for the quality of his products, including a gold medal at the 22nd Exposition Internationale Culinaire d'Alimentation & d'Hygiène in Paris in 1905. For 20 years, from 1895 to 1915, the revenue of the firm went from 88,000 to 4.6 million Finnish marks.[26] The corporate culture was embedded in Christian values, since Karl Fazer was a strong believer in the Protestant Work Ethic from his Swiss heritage.[27]

Inter-War Dynasties

One of the most prominent Finnish dynasties from the interwar years is the Herlin family. The first step had already been taken by the time entrepreneur Harald Herlin became the owner of Kone, currently a world-leading manufacturer of lifts and escalators, in 1924. Licensed by Graham Brothers, the subsidiary of Gottfrid Strömberg Oy imported and installed lifts, transitioning to production in 1918. Indebtedness and poor demand in the wake of the post-war recession, however, hurtled the parent company into a financial crisis. When consulted by the bank, Herlin determined that the subsidiary's assets would cover the parent company's debts and worked out a deal with the previous owner. Kone was now fully independent with Herlin firmly at the reins. The company relocated to an old margarine plant and ratcheted up production from 200 to 320 lifts the first year. After obtaining a board post and going to school in Finland, Germany and the United States, his son Heikki took over as managing director at the age of 31. The fast track to the top was clearly staked out—he acquired all the skills and experience he needed from the leading enterprises and universities of the time.[28]

As production flowered in the 1930s to include cranes, he took advantage of his technical and language skills to woo the export market. The equipment was vital to reconstruction of cities flattened by the war. Kone benefitted especially from the demand by the Soviet Union that Finland pay reparations as the price for peace. The Finnish government subsidized the export of 108 lifts, 202 cranes and 265 hoists from 1945 to 1952. Demand for Kone products skyrocketed in the wave of modernization that swept across industrialized nations during the 1950s and 1960s, spurring the construction of office buildings, department stores and hospitals.[29]

The younger Herlin was a member of independent Finland's first industrial magnate generation, though reflecting the epoch of the country squire if not a patriarchal figure in his own right. Kone was still a small business when he first stood at the helm, and his entrepreneurial talents provided the impetus that a new relationship with technology and the market demanded. His genius was the ability to spur new demand by being constantly on the lookout for new products, flexing his muscles with the competition and being rewarded with a dynamic export business in the process. He turned over the managing director post to his son Pekka in 1964 but held on to the chairmanship until 1987.[30]

The Ehrnrooths were another Finnish family that built a dynasty in the years leading up to World War II. Unlike the Herlins, they were seasoned warriors of national politics, nobility that had played an important military role. Major General Gustaf Adolf Ehrnrooth fought on the side of Sweden in the 1808–1809 war and was exalted in Lieutenant Stål's legends for his feats. His son Casimir, a military expert for the Russian Czar, served as Minister of War in Bulgaria, which was under Russian control at the time, during the 1880s. Regimental Commander Adolf Ehrnrooth, his grandnephew, was among the country's heroes during the 1941–1944 Continuation War. On the civilian side, the family has held top positions in the Finnish private sector for a century and a half.

Carl Albert Ehrnrooth laid the foundation of the dynasty in the midnineteenth century when he bought the family estate at Sesta and started a large-scale agricultural and forestry business. His son Axel, who studied law and learned banking on the job in London, became managing director and one of the principal shareholders at Private Bank. A magnet for investments by Finland-Swedish interests, it became the fifth largest bank in the country before succumbing to the currency crisis and recession that followed World War I. Ehrnrooth dusted off his breeches, founded the first Finnish development company and sat on the boards of countless manufacturers until his death in 1950.

His brother George exhibited similar entrepreneurial and networking skills, starting a number of businesses while managing the agricultural and forestry holdings that his dad had passed down. He founded several research organizations, not to mention the Agricultural Bank (1910), which eventually underwent two mergers and attracted a growing coterie of customers. By the end of the decade, he had acquired a fortune in the stock market, boosted by galloping inflation but not wholly consumed by the post-war recession. Fascinated by engine technology, particularly fast cars, he collaborated with the government to lay the groundwork for the Finnish civil aviation industry.[31]

The family wealth received a welcome shot in the arm when Göran, his youngest son, married Louise von Julin from an extraordinarily well-to-do family that owned Fiskars, a leading manufacturer. After obtaining a law degree, he joined the Nordic Cooperative Bank, the new harbour for Finland Swedish industrial assets, in 1933. He never worked anywhere else for the rest of his life. From his perch there, he controlled much of the Finnish private sector in the 1970s and onwards. As managing director at the bank, he was on the boards of many manufacturers. Fiskars, which made scissors and knives, Kaukas (forestry), FÅÅ (shippers, later to become Silja Line) and Wärtsilä (engineering) were among the family businesses. As a board member, he represented both the creditor and the controlling interest.[32]

Entrepreneurship in the Countryside of Jutland

The archetypical Danish industrial firm in the 1930s was a small family-run corporation that produced machines or goods for the agricultural sector. A mechanic, foremost in the countryside of Jutland, who had some experience of other small workshops, had founded it. The owners of these firms seemed to have a shared vision of making use of new technologies in order to increase the productivity of famers. Since the Great Depression was tackled by protectionism, like import bans, they could expand thanks to the absence of international competition. After the Depression, lower prices of energy and the modernization of society made them quite profitable.[33]

Among these start-ups, Danfoss became a world leader in heating and cooling technology (thermostats, compressors and automated control systems). The name comes from water flowing out of a valve (foss). The founder Mads Clausen was the youngest son of a farmer and in the workshop behind the farmhouse, his interest in mechanics began to grow. His great grandfather ran the workshop; the young Clausen observed the production of pumps and spinning wheels and noticed the importance of craftsmanship and good quality. During shorter periods of employment, after having graduated from Odense Technical School, he experimented with expansion valves for refrigeration systems and, favoured by an import ban on valves from the United States, he took the chance to set up his own.[34]

In 1932, Clausen made his first valve and started small production on behalf of his employer. Since he preferred to have all control to himself, he returned to his old boyhood attic, where he assembled valves and pressure-tested them in a bathtub in the middle of the floor. There was a demand for his unique product, and in 1933 he sold 466 valves, at a value of 1,700 euros.[35] A factory was set up and by the end of World War II, the firm had 200 employees. Thereafter, the workforce increased substantially and went from 1,000 people in 1953 to 7,000 in 1970. The construction of new factories around the family estate had a major impact on the population and infrastructure of the municipality.[36]

The background of the mechanical engineering firm Grundfos was much the same, a breakthrough innovation and a wish by founder Poul Due Jensen to set up his own workshop, after having worked for others for a while. In 1943, the family bought land behind his house in Bjerringbro in Jutland and started planning a factory in the backyard. Four years later, Due Jensen introduced unique products within circulation pumps and central heating, and in 1949, the family business began exporting. The reason his business grow more than others seems to have been his determination to solve mechanical problems and satisfy customers. He seems to have had an almost unique ability to solve mechanical problems, which came in handy when he got his first order for a pump installation in 1945. Circulation pumps would later go to worldwide export. Another innovation that broke with industry logic and hastened the modernization of society was central heating. As in the case of Danfoss, demand increased substantially after World War II. New plants in Denmark and abroad, product development, growing exports and recruitments of employees met this demand.[37]

The innovation in Lego was to certain degree the result of teamwork between father and son. Suffering from the Great Depression, carpenter Ole Kirk Kristiansen started to produce wooden toys instead of houses because nobody in the village of Billund could afford to pay for a new house or for the renovation of an existing on. The idea of producing toys came from a society for promoting Danish articles, Landsforeningen Dansk Arbjede. His personal situation was severe for two reasons: creditors had started to demand cash for collateral and Ole Kirk was living alone with his four children, after the sudden death of his wife in 1931. If there had been a social security system in Denmark at the time, my father would never have been forced to redirect his profession, his son Godtfred declared later. Poverty triggered the family to start thinking of alternative ways to survive, and with hand-made drawings and inspiration from Godtfred and his three brothers, their hope went to wooden toys. The name Lego was taken from the Danish words *leg godt* (play well). At that time, the founders were not aware that Lego was the Latin expression for gathering and putting together. The moral values of the family were based on Christianity (the Protestant Ethic) and Ole Kirk held morning prayers for his employees in the carpentry workshop.[38]

The demand for wooden toys was increasing and in 1943, production employed 40 people. To produce wooden toys was not much of an innovation, though. The break with industry logic came after World War II, when Ole Kirk and his son Godtfred began forming plastic bricks in a machine imported from England and with technical assistance from the Danish government-owned Technological Institute. The machine for plastic injection moulding was the first of its kind for the production of plastic toys in Denmark. Since the machine was quite expensive—a 50% higher than the earnings of the business in 1946—and moulded plastic toys aroused little appreciation in England, it was a risky project.[39]

The family was not convinced that the bricks would ever conquer wooden toys. Thus, the break with industry logic and profits may have caused some surprise even for the innovator. In 1951, "Automatic Binding Bricks" was marketed as a separate product, aside from wooden toys.

In 1955, the bricks were linked to a set of repeated creativity, as a system of play for both sexes and all ages where the various products could be used together rather than being one-off toys. The more bricks you had, the more you could build, which offered true appeal to the homo ludens. As mentioned earlier, if there had been an extensive social welfare system in the 1930s, it is unlikely that Ole Kirk would have laid the foundations of a dynasty. The efforts by the Kristiansen family and the success story of Lego underline the saying that necessity is the mother of invention.[40]

Post-War Dynasties

Many dynasties were founded in the early post-war period, during the transition to a mature industrial society. During the 1950s and 1960s, new businesses emerged as a response to the modernization of society and efforts to rationalize the distribution of goods for mass consumption. Some of the emerging dynasties from this period brought not so much technological innovations as new ideas within logistics, value chains, customer benefit and marketing. That is true of Ikea, where a new distribution system was the key invention. Ingvar Kamprad's insights as an entrepreneur and furniture dealer were profound and extended over more than half a century. In his detailed handbook, *A Furniture Dealer's Testament*, he emphasized the importance of having a range of goods clearly identified as part of a profiled trademark. A basic rule is to offer a wide range of household furnishings of appropriate design and function at prices so low that as many people in the world as possible consider them affordable. At the start, every traditional competitor tried to marginalize Kamprad, who then put up a production line in Poland to pursue the visionary idea of inexpensive furniture.

The innovation of Ikea concerns the establishment of a trademark that emphasizes the importance of creating team spirit and an atmosphere in which customers, suppliers and co-workers feel that they all are responsible for the outcome. The idea is to give the impression that everyone is a stakeholder. Comparisons with a soccer team are relevant. The leader may have the duty to develop and encourage his players, but each of them also has an obligation to help to improve the team as a whole. Ingvar Kamprad argued that people should be viewed as pillars of society:

> Take care of our social pillars! These are the simple, quiet and straightforward people, who are always willing to lend a hand. They perform their duty and accept their responsibilities without being seen. For them, areas of responsibility are a necessary, but unfortunate, concept. For them, supporting the entire organization is as obvious as helping out and always sharing.[41]

Kamprad was an extraordinary pioneer, a catalyst for a whole new worldview in his industry. He unfurled an unprecedented global brand of entrepreneurship and shaped a distinctly Swedish corporate culture that is now recognized the world. It all started when the 17-year-old sat in his mother's kitchen and assembled his first collapsible milking stools. When she fretted about the 12 stools he hoped to sell, he reassured her, "Just you wait, one day the whole world will be sitting on a stool from Småland."[42]

Much later he recalled,

> The years that the furniture industry boycotted me left an indelible impression. I concluded that negative promotion and advertising never pay off. The problem with my counterparts were that they tried to hold things back and keep them from seeing the light of day instead of coming up with constructive ideas of their own. Who knows whether we would have been so successful had they competed honestly and above board? It was their only chance to stop us.[43]

Kamprad infuriated an entire industry, herded together a flock of enthusiastic employees and embarked on a new approach to manufacturing and marketing household items. Instead of fighting for more favourable business and fiscal regulations, Kamprad lost no time in challenging his competitors by locating a large percentage of production abroad, starting with Poland. He was unencumbered by any kind of government monopoly, and the highly profitable business was not reliant on venture capital or the heavily regulated credit market.

His most striking innovation was cost consciousness: frugality is his lesson to the ages. Not only did the company design its own merchandise, but it incorporated simplicity and inexpensiveness of manufacture into their very concept. Production of components or entire items was outsourced to countries with low labour costs and suppliers that were highly specialized under Ikea's watchful eye. The large-scale approach held prime costs down to a minimum.

Catalogues for consumers, as well as self-service at large department stories built on relatively cheap suburban land, greased sales. Manufacturing techniques that allowed the goods to be packed in flat containers for home assembly saved even more money when it came to distribution and storage. As a result, Kamprad was able to offer 20%–30% discounts off traditional furniture dealers.[44]

Society Modernizes

The son of a pastor, Villum Kann Rasmussen was the founder of a highly innovative and profitable family business who grew up in Mandø off the west coast of Jutland. After engineering studies and a few youthful jobs, he and a classmate went into the wind power business together. But potential customers were few and far between, so he turned to natural lighting and obtained a patent for galvanized bars to be used in windows and glass ceilings. This was the precursor of V. Kann Rasmussen & Co., which he founded in 1941, and its Velux window breakthrough.[45]

Timing is everything. Interest in natural lighting had been on the rise since the 1930s. Henry Ford hade had maintained that it was a cost saver, especially when trying to boost productivity. The Danish Minister of Education was an advocate for brighter classrooms. Converted lofts grew popular during the lean war years. Rasmussen's novel window design created a market of its own in a world crying for modernization—sales rose tenfold in the immediate post-war years. The plant at Horsens on the east coast of Jutland saturated the Danish market and the time came to expand. Taking advantage of his quality products and networking abilities, he and a business partner build up a sales organization across the length and breadth of West Germany. By the early 1960s, they had 10 times as many customers there as back home.[46]

The modernization of Swedish society spurred many entrepreneurs in the building and construction industry, where Lars Erik Lundberg in Norrköping came to stand at the forefront of a new industry logic. The idea of the firm Byggnads AB L E Lundberg in Norrköping was to build houses in stock and wait for buyers to show up. This enables them to utilize their fixed resources even when the business cycle shifted downwards, which compensated for the swings in the highly fluctuating housing market. The common business model in the building business in the 1950s and 1960s was to sell off once the house was constructed. Lundberg, however, developed a business for real estate parallel to the construction business and used the profits from the latter to invest in the property market. Rents, which provided steady revenue to count on, made the overall business less vulnerable to unfavourable business cycles.[47]

The business model got off to a flying start thanks to a push in the market for multi-storey dwellings. The Social Democratic government launched a programme in 1965 to produce 1 million residences over 10 years, a target that was reached. The government stimulated production in many ways within the framework of extensive housing policy, and Lundberg went from town to town to acquire land set for aside for building. After the period of construction of multi-storey dwellings had peaked in the early 1970s, they stayed strong in the markets of small houses and commercial buildings. When the second generation of the family took over in the mid-1970s, they started to develop a portfolio of industrial stocks, in order to reduce the risks of the volatile property market, where activity had slowed down. During the following decades, the family created a diversified investment company of substantial market value.[48]

In 1945, Kosti Oras, Erkki Paasikivi and his wife Irja, daughter of Kosti, started an engineering company. The location was Rauma, a small village on the west coast of Finland, north of Turko (Åbo). A workshop was set up in the cellar of the apartment building where they all lived. Typically for family companies, work and leisure overlapped and the three sons of the Passikivis, who later took key positions in the business, followed dealings closely from their childhood. The start-up capital came from earnings of bus operations run by Kosti Oras, who took four-fifths of the shares and gave his name to the company—Oras. However, it was the younger Erkki Passikivi, trained as an engineer, who developed the new company.[49]

After having manufactured a range of product singly or in small series, the breakthrough came when Oras started to produce two-handle faucets. The push came from the urbanization and modernization of homes at a time when most residences had only cold water on tap and had to heat it themselves for washing. Because of the rudimentary water supply system, there was demand of all kinds of fittings, including radiator valves, and Oras started to provide these products. The entrepreneurial spirit of Passikivi led him to West Germany, since he was not satisfied with the casting fitting methods in Finland. He used his networking capacity to transfer technology and knowledge from a German firm. By licensing the German casting method, Oras achieved many advantages in relation to other Scandinavian producers regarding both quality and cost-effectiveness. Thanks to his German business relationships, the firm continue to grow even when import controls in West Europe were lifted in 1957. Gradually, control of the firm shifted from Erkki Paasikivi to his three sons, which strengthened the position of the firm internationally by acquisition and collaboration. As of the late 1990s, the family started to invest in other industries and became the largest private shareholder in three major Finnish companies: Kemira, Uponor and Tikkurila. In the mid-2010s, Oras was Europe's fourth largest manufacturer of indoor faucets, operated by Annika Passikivi in the third generation.[50]

Family-Based Retailers

The founder of H&M, Erling Persson, illustrates a distinctive way of breaking with industry logic. His entrepreneurial ideas were concrete, down-to-earth and focused on business models within the apparel industry. He declared that inventories of unsold goods are both risky and expensive and should therefore be avoided as far as possible. The original business model of efficient and high-volume stores was American, and he transferred this idea to Sweden after a trip to the United States following World War II.

When Persson set up his company in Västerås in 1947, he stressed the importance of a strong financial position to survive future challenges. In his "Testimony of an Underwear Dealer," his concern was how marketing and selling should be organized to reach optimal results. He stressed the importance of being able to read other people's minds and made suggestions on how to carry out negotiations efficiently. The entrepreneurial aspect was contained in Erling Persson's concept of *controlled imagination*, which was presented together with an admonition to find co-workers who were *constructively creative* and had the ability to implement their ideas. For the family, it is a matter of utilizing its network capacity and of providing space for visionary—not utopian—co-workers, following arguments from the founder of H&M.[51]

Erling and his son Stefan Persson showed the importance of listening to customers, but also had the courage to pursue their own ideas. The desire to create something new was manifested in choosing various design programmes, for example by hiring a fashion star such as Stella McCartney. Like all successful entrepreneurs, the Perssons have been motivated by curiosity and considerable self-confidence. Like Kamprad in Ikea, the Persson family violated accepted ideas and brought a new approach to the business. Both Kamprad and Persson created new markets that did not exist before there companies started. Their organizations and products have repeatedly been reorganized to aim at new goals. H&M started to use what has been called value chains, where control of the underlying delivery systems aims to reduce costs and maintain low consumer prices. By eliminating middlemen and integrating backwards, H&M became its own wholesaler, while resource supplements were systematically devoted to investments and geographic expansion. To lower costs further, production of clothing was relocated to low-wage countries in southern Europe and Asia.[52]

Entrepreneurial leadership in the Persson family was based on simplicity, anti-bureaucratic principles and a rejection of academic cleverness. In this regard, they are very similar to Kamprad's pragmatic business ideas of how a firm should be built up and expanded worldwide. There are also similarities to how Ruben Rausing steered the expansion of Tetra Pak, another emerging dynasty founded in the post-war period. These three dynasties also had another thing in common: they were a response to the need to streamline the distribution of goods for mass consumption during the 1950s and 1960s.

H&M offered fashionable clothes at reasonable prices as an alternative to expensive trademark items. Marketing was based on aggressive exhibits and advertising, as well as on stores with large display windows in the best locations of Swedish cities. Ikea delivered their products in flat packages and saved on delivery while passing on other costs to customers. The innovation from Tetra Pak—the tightly closed milk carton—also resulted in a distinct simplification of distribution. However, in other regards the vision of Rausing deviated from the first two, since activity at Tetra Pak followed the engineering tradition within the classical Swedish mechanical manufacturing industry.[53]

Tetra Pak traces its history back to Åkerlund & Rausing, which grew to become the leading national packager in the 1930s. Packaging of merchandise that had previously been sold loose streamlined purchasing and distribution in the spirit of modernization. Smart young employees headed for the United States to spy on inventions that could be adapted in Lund to the Swedish way of doing things. The next challenge in the quest for consumables that could be pre-packaged was to find more economical ways of delivering milk, the perishable item par excellence. Gothenburg and Stockholm had latched onto the concept of bottles, but sale by the weight at separate dairy outlets was still the norm. Rausing instructed Holger Crafoord, his right-hand man, to bring back samples of the cartons that had been launched in America so Swedish labs could analyze how they had been constructed. But the government had slapped a ceiling on milk containers in order to protect consumers and the paper products were much too expensive for the Swedish market. Åkerlund & Rausing management faced the daunting task of coming up with materials and production processes that would enable extraordinarily cost-effective disposable cartons.[54]

The tetrahedron that emerged from their efforts earned the ultimate tribute when physics titan Niels Bohr paid a visit to the Lund plant and called it "a perfect practical application of a mathematical problem."[55] Erik Wallenberg, the inventor, had no choice but to cede proprietary rights to Rausing, ablaze with personal pride in the discovery, not to mention dynastic ambitions. Rausing continued down the same path, applying for every patent in his own name and occasionally talking himself into believing that he was the actual inventor. His obstinacy led to predictable disputes and bad blood in the organization.[56]

Tetra Pak first became profitable in the 1960s after having been essentially insolvent and on the brink of collapse had it not been for the financial strength of the parent company, loans from SEB and the absence of a balance sheet for liquidation purposes. Following a major acquisition, the Tetra Laval Group was worth more than SEK 80 billion in the mid-1990s. The company sold 84 billion tetrahedral packages every year and did business in 163 countries. But it suffered a number of self-inflicted wounds along the way, particularly Rausing's knee-jerk opposition to anything that might stand trip up his dynastic ambitions a la the Wallenbergs. As young inexperienced men, his sons Gad and Hans joined the executive team but offered scanty, if not downright toxic, leadership in the eyes of their employees. Uninhibited by the rules of fair play, Rausing gradually elbowed out his competitors while ignoring Marcus Wallenberg's advice that he list the company so that more venture capital would be at his disposal. Be that as it may, he ended up selling Åkerlund & Rausing to Wallenberg's Swedish Match, relieving financial pressure and clearing the way for investment. Ultimately he showed Crafoord the door as well and set the stage for a true family dynasty blissfully independent of the stock market.[57]

A strong incentive to start a family company is to strike out on its own. That was the reason trained shoemaker Karl Toosbuy quit his job at a factory in Copenhagen to settle down with his wife and five-year-old daughter Hanni in a small village near the German border, where he started Ecco. The decision to start production in the sleepy agricultural town Bredebro with just over 1,000 inhabitants was strategic, according to his daughter. "My father wasn't good at having a boss. He wanted to do things on his own. He also didn't want to base the business in Copenhagen, partly because he felt the workforce would be more stable outside of the city. So he chose Bredebro."[58] His innovative idea was to make shoes that fit, which sounds simple, but meant a break with industry logic, since his shoes were more flexible, light and comfortable than other exclusive footwear. The price at the retailer was a little above average for the mass market but within reach of a wide range of consumers.

After 15 years of struggling with bad financial performance, the "Joke" shoe succeeded in the market and was followed by innovative brands like "Free," "Time" and "Soft." Ecco was among the first to stamp the name and logo of the company on the soles—to leave footprints around the world—which subsequently became a regular design feature among many brands. The founder did not only pioneer in craftsmanship and design but also by taking control of every step in the production process, from the cow to the consumer. This vertical integration process was necessary to guarantee high quality. The tanneries of Ecco later became suppliers of leather to the fashion, sports and automotive industries. In 2013, employees at Ecco numbered 18,500.[59]

Into the Digital Revolution

In the Stenbeck dynasty, Hugo Stenbeck met Wilhelm Klingspor and Robert von Horn and started a business together in 1936. Klingspor and von Horn, noble landlords and conservative politicians in the countryside of Sweden, contributed the capital while Counsel Stenbeck was the smart businessman with a solid network in competitive Stockholm. After the Kreuger Crash in 1932, Stenbeck was questioned in his role as former advisor to Ivar Kreuger—the Match King—but was able to keep up his reputation among the elite of capitalists. The core holdings in the new company Kinnevik, the name taken from a bay in Lake Vänern, were estates in Eastern and Western Gothia, a confectionary manufacturer and the forest company Korsnäs, the latter becoming a cash cow for many decades to come. Kinnevik was based on the liquidation of a sugar company, which generated a substantial profit and seed capital for further investment. Hugo Stenbeck started to invest in new companies with the explicit target of making money for the three families, and was successful as a long-term committed owner of industrial interests.[60]

Sometimes the break with industry logic in the second generation of a dynasty is more fundamental than the initial one. Jan Stenbeck, the son of Hugo Stenbeck, was born to an entrepreneurial environment and took control of family ownership in Kinnevik after a bitter power struggle within the family. As a resident of New York and with an MBA from

Harvard, he transferred a competitive market-oriented corporate culture to Sweden, abetted by his own aggressive style of leadership. He challenged two regulated lines of business—commercialized television and telecommunications—and was able to break up both state monopolies. As an example of blunt methods, on New Year Eve in 1987 he introduced a commercial television channel by satellite from London to Scandinavia, after having identified a loophole in national legislation.

Gradually, Kinnevik went from a traditional investment company with core holdings in primary industries to one of the most expansive listed companies, focusing on emerging industries. According to his business model, Jan Stenbeck showed that new technology will always beat ideas, venture capital as well as politics. Or as the founder of Intel Andy Grove put it: "What can be done, will be done." Jan Stenbeck made friends with leading Social Democrats and subsequently convinced the labour movement in Sweden that all citizens would benefit from de-monopolization and the right of free establishment.[61]

While protests by proponents of government ownership and heavy regulation were legion, even leading Social Democrats gradually warmed to the advantages of choice and unabashed free enterprise. Other leading elected officials were swept along in the tsunami of deregulation that roared across the Atlantic and ambushed a Scandinavian model that had appeared to be cast in stone.

Stenbeck's sixth sense led him to fresh sources of surplus earnings that he could reinvest in a series of entrepreneurial enterprises, which completely reshuffled the private sector. He had shown that the sky's the limit, that the prudent marriage of ground-breaking technology and venture capital can reshape the political map. He baptized Sweden in the most aggressive of American capitalist credos and upended all previous calculi.

Countryside Origins

Most dynasties started in the countryside, or at least outside the largest cities of the Nordic countries. The innovations were part of the transformation of the economy from an agriculture to a modern industrial society. The wealth of some of the oldest dynasties reflects the potential profits embedded in the exploitation and export of natural resources. The operations of the oldest dynasties were based on craftsmanship. Thus, the firms were dependent on a loyal and skilled workforce to be trained internally, in contrast to well-educated people from academia. To be dependent on local workers put pressure on the behaviour of the founder, who had to appear as trustworthy in order to obtain the loyalty and long-term commitment of workers.

Capital expenditures on plants and premises carried a lower price tag in rural areas than in the big cities. Ditto for personnel costs. Generally speaking, a new business could reckon with the support of the local community, which translated into a loyal workforce. A college education was a needless frill given that most production was based on artisanship, machine design and the wholesale/retail sector. Skills development was an in-house matter rooted in long practical experience such that there was little incentive to switch jobs, particularly when robust organic growth promised steady career advancement. Employee turnover could normally be kept to a minimum.

Researchers have found that the employees of family businesses are willing to sacrifice some of their potential pay check for an implicit assurance that their positions will be safe even when the business cycle dips. Such steadfast devotion had already become a staple of the entrepreneurial economy in the nineteenth century. The family was expected to exercise foresight and save for a rainy day. Having to lay people off was a blemish on the honour of the owners. Many founders were devout Christians and embodied the Protestant Ethic in their approach to running a company. Their concern for workers was palpable even though salaries were considerably lower than in the cities, and they contributed generously to community organizations. The allegiance of the local population was greater than the need to meet the demands of banks and a better educated labour pool in the urban areas.

This chapter looks at founders of family businesses and the needs they identified among the general public. Their genius of their innovations and business methods was the ability to satisfy such needs while edging out the potential competition. In an eternal dance with technology and history, individual entrepreneurs spurred the economic transformations that accompanied the transition from agricultural to industrial to information society. Particularly since national markets were limited by their very nature, the earliest dynasties benefitted from strong Nordic demand for natural resources. The entrepreneurship of the later dynasties targeted domestic consumers instead, while exports of their goods and services took off at a subsequent stage.

Production satisfied widespread needs and could be ramped up at narrowing margins as demand grew. Those who lived and did business in the rural areas and who participated directly in the mechanization of the agricultural economy were in the best position to identify such needs. They jump-started the transition to industrial society. The growth of new structures would have been stymied had it not been for their zeal and determination. The personal entrepreneurship that began to strike root in the years leading up to World War II was also based in the rural areas with their tradition of craftsmanship complemented by an expanding wholesale and retail sector for the goods and services they offered. Efficient exploitation of available resources permitted the families to mould the future of many key Nordic industries.

The individuals who presided over the dynasties that survived were at the cutting edge of meeting a host of needs that consumers were experiencing in their daily lives, both at home and in the community. Their innovative approaches and forward-looking leadership paved the way for new mass markets that they themselves were in the process of begetting. They set things up for future generations to remain one step ahead in the market even as their monopolies fell by the wayside. By the time globalization settled in, many of them had established a nigh-unto insurmountable lead by virtue of their solid origins, networks and customer relationships (historical anchor). Rural communities were a hothouse for initiative and expansion that made family businesses a growing force to reckon with throughout the Nordic countries.

Notes

1. Sandberg (1979).
2. Hornby (1988), pp. 24–5 and Ellemose (2004), pp. 15–16.
3. Hornby (1988), pp. 33–41 and Ellemose (2004), pp. 17–19.
4. Schybergson (1992), p. 82.
5. Schybergson (1992), p. 30.
6. Schybergson (1992), p. 79.
7. Magretta (1998).
8. Ojala and Pajunen (2006), p. 170.
9. Sejersted (2002), pp. 220–40; 472.
10. Sogner (2012), pp. 21–96 and Thue (2008), pp. 394–416.
11. Sogner (2001), pp. 254–7; 282–3.
12. Sogner (2001), pp. 9–53; 277–86.
13. De Geer (1998), pp. 15–16.
14. Mattsson (1984), pp. 21–60.
15. De Geer (1998), pp. 20–43 and Ericson (1982), pp. 13–25.
16. Hauge (1993), pp. 13–41.
17. Hauge (1993), pp. 42–75.
18. Glete (1994), p. 134–7.
19. Nilsson (2005), pp. 163–5.
20. Nilsson (2005). In the 1860s, commercial banking developed rapidly, encouraged by the wave of liberal economic policies and the monetarisation of the capital market. The 1864 banking law allowed not only unrestricted interest rates, but also the right to set up joint stock banks and establish branches in cities other than where the head office was located. In the following year, eight new joint stock banks were set up. Sjögren (2008), pp. 31–2.
21. Sjögren (2008), p. 26.
22. Sundin (2002), pp. 15–18.
23. Norland (2011a), pp. 14–48.
24. Norland (2011a), p. 38.
25. Hoving (1951), pp. 20–5; www.fazer.com/fazer-since-1891
26. Hoving (1951), pp. 26–43.
27. Donner (1991), p. 53.
28. Biografiskt lexikon för Finland; www.kone.com/en/company/history/.
29. www.kone.com/en/company/history/.
30. Biografiskt lexikon för Finland.
31. Biografiskt lexikon för Finland; Nikander (1929).
32. Biografiskt lexikon för Finland; SvD Näringsliv (2002).
33. Iversen and Andersen (2008), pp. 298–303.

34. The Danfoss Story (2010).
35. The Danfoss Story (2010).
36. Boje and Johansen (1995) and The Danfoss Story (2010).
37. Grundfos (1992), pp. 41–60; 75–7 and Ballisager (2007).
38. Cortzen (1996), pp. 27–42; Hansen (1997).
39. Cortzen (1996), pp. 31; 41; 46 and Iversen and Andersen (2008), p. 309.
40. Cortzen (1996), pp. 50; 70.
41. Torekull (2006), pp. 336–9.
42. Torekull (2011), left cover.
43. Torekull (2011), p. 63.
44. Björk (1998), p. 16.
45. Boje (2004), pp. 11–113.
46. Boje (2004), pp. 112–93.
47. Ekegren (1994), p. 31.
48. Ekegren (1994), pp. 31–73.
49. Herranen (2015), pp. 12–23.
50. Herranen (2015), pp. 25–195.
51. Pettersson (2001), pp. 299–316.
52. Pettersson (2001), pp. 315–16.
53. Pettersson (2001), p. 314.
54. Andersson and Larsson (1998), pp. 1–23; 76 and Rydenfelt (1995), pp. 26–33.
55. Andersson and Larsson (1998), p. 13.
56. Andersson and Larsson (1998).
57. Sjögren (2012), pp. 324–32 and Andersson and Larsson (1998), p. 279 and pp. 324–5.
58. Family Business Yearbook (2014), pp. 38–9.
59. Family Business Yearbook (2014), pp. 39–40.
60. Björk (2006), pp. 72–99 and Andersson (2000), pp. 147–53.
61. Andersson (2000), pp. 16; 28–41 and Björk (2006), pp. 265–78.

4   Strategy, Structure and Dynamics

When a company starts off with a specific innovation in mind, the industry in which it will do business is generally a given. Adding the founder's visions of governance to the mix helps define the parameters (historical anchor) for his children and grandchildren to operate within. Most dynasties offer the same kinds of goods and services from one generation to the next. A.P. Møller-Mærsk has been faithful to the shipping industry for four generations and the Olsen family for five. The Perssons buy and sell clothing just as Erling, their forbear, did in the 1950s and 1960s. Dan Olsson owns ships on the west coast of Sweden in the footsteps of his father and his father before him. The Bonniers have published and sold books and periodicals in Sweden and abroad for six generations. The Schibsteds have played a similar role in the Norwegian media market. Four Danish families have devoted their lives to plastic toys, thermostats, compressors and pumps respectively. When it comes to Finland, the Herlins have been in the lift and crane business for four generations, the Ahlströms have never strayed from engineering and the Fazers are just as sweet on candy.

The pattern holds for the vast majority of dynasties. Which isn't to say that the original innovation does not evolve with the times—to wit, Ikea's distribution system, Tetra Pak's mathematical refinement and H&M's advertising genius. The largest and most dynamic family businesses have continually taken their initial concept and run with it to new areas of excellence and application.

Stick to What You Know, or Not

The maxim might be "sticking to what you know," but there are a number of exceptions to that norm. The enterprises within the Stenbeck sphere have moved further and further away from their original core activity, while forestry, mechanical engineering and finance nowadays complement the original real estate holdings in the case of the Lundberg family. The Andresen family has left the tobacco industry, for 149 years a core holding and cash cow. With fresh money, they initiated collaborative projects between public and private interests, as philanthropic endeavours and a microfinance institution aiming to stimulate growth in impoverished countries. In most dynasties, the change of direction happens after a shift at the top of the organization, when younger members of the family get an opportunity to try out their ideas.

Most dynasties are vertically and horizontally integrated. But when it comes to investment in activities without links to the core business—diversification—the pattern is not consistent. There are less diversified and strongly diversified ones, and their relation to performance is not given in advance. There have been dynasties that have stuck to what they already know, i.e., stayed less diversified, but have ended up as losers financially, while others, thanks to their expansion outside their core holdings, have strengthened their long-run positions as family-based groups. In the former category, we have Broström, Kiær and Solberg and Saléninvest, while the latter type is illustrated by the Andresen, Johnson, Lundberg and Stenbeck families. There are also families that have developed into business groups, where coordination is the mechanism linking separate industrial holdings together, as for example the Ehrnrooths, Olsens, Møller-Mærsks and Wallenbergs.

Another type of industrial dynamic is seen in the case of Bonnier and Lego. After having broadened their industrial interests, they experienced substantial losses and forced themselves back to basics. Many dynasties have diversified but retain a strong focus on the core business, as Ahlström, Danfoss, Grundfos, Fazer, Ikea, Ecco and Oras. They have continuously upgraded the original product and process innovations made by the first generation of the family. The challenge has been to enter new markets outside their small domestic base. In that respect, they have not stuck to what they already know. They have been able to challenge new international markets and have become world-leading exporters thanks to their unique innovations.

A Structural Evolutionary Pattern

The structural changes of the dynasties in the twentieth century have followed the general evolution in the Western world. First diversification through the formation of conglomerates that was then reversed through corporate pruning and outsourcing resulted in a return to the emphasis on core competence and activities. Viewing these changes in the enterprise structure from World War II until the beginning of the twenty-first century reveals a chain of cause and effect. The strict legislation against increased concentration in the economy during the 1950s resulted in a diversified and decentralized group structure. Conglomerates were the extreme examples of this tendency. They were praised both by theoreticians and practical businessmen, not least for levelling out liquidity fluctuations thanks to investment in countercyclical industries. The strongly diversified group was considered by many to be the ultimate form of enterprise organization.

The initiatives in Northern Europe were inspired by the success story of multi-divisional firms and the new management ideas in the United States. Soon experts reported that European firms were catching up with their American counterparts in the race to establish divisional corporate structures. While the share of large multidivisional firms in North America had risen from 20% to 77% in 1949–1969, the shares of Germany, France, Italy and Great Britain had reached 40%, 43%, 26% and 70% respectively. These developments were taken as evidence that multidivisional firms were in the process of outmanoeuvring all other forms of corporate organization.[1]

Conglomerates had their own theoretical rationale and a major impact on corporate organization in the Western world. A corporation might sell 20% of its products and services to the aviation, chemical and construction industry each, 10% to the clothing industry, and the remaining 30% to five additional industries. The idea was that diversification of risk and profitability went hand in hand. However, by the beginning of the 1970s, research found that companies had done better when they maintained their focus on the core business. The lack of an overall strategy or clear relationship between the various business areas became an insurmountable obstacle. Case after case illustrated the impracticability of combining profitability and heavy diversification, while M-shaped, division-based organizations were here to stay.[2]

The pendulum swung back in the direction of increased focus on core activities, with the hope of improving resource utilization and increasing profits. The new mottos were outsourcing, back to basics and downsizing. Profits largely depended not on productivity increases, but the purchase and sale of firms, first by creating diversified companies and then by dismantling them. In terms of corporate control, the centre of gravity shifted from independent management to institutional investors who demanded short-term results. Most of the new investors had no interest in active industrial ownership. The turnover of ownership capital became increasingly rapid and was used less and less as a tool for long-term value creation.[3]

Conglomerates—a Blind Alley

Many Nordic firms followed the American pattern and became increasingly diversified. Among them were Wallenberg-owned companies such as Swedish Match and Astra, but also firms without long-term committed owners but strong leadership, such as Volvo (Procordia). The American norm, however, was far from new. A large family business that had started to diversify at an early stage was the Johnson Group. During Consul-General Axel Ax:son Johnson's time, the second generation after the founder and entrepreneur Axel Johnson, the enterprise expanded into a very diverse group of firms. In the interwar years, traditional trading activity was complemented with industrial, transportation and building firms.

This pattern was common among traditional merchant houses. During the generation under mining engineer Axel Ax:son Johnson, the group was effectively a conglomerate, at a time when foreign expansion was eagerly pursued by the family. As a conglomerate, the Johnson Group experienced severe difficulties in the 1980s when world market competition for raw materials, petroleum and steel stiffened. The Group lacked the resources to match the competition's investments and production capacity. As a result, the conglomerate was broken up when its industrial commitments were pruned, thus freeing up resources that had been tied up in long-term fixed assets. As an example, Nordstjernan was transformed from a closed family industrial conglomerate to a listed Nordic construction and real estate company (NCC).[4]

The changeover to a core activity without industrial connections was a thorough and dramatic process in the long history of the Johnson family. In contrast to several other shipping companies during the structural crisis of the 1970s, the Johnson Group never became insolvent and was able to retain its independence. It was, however, a close call: leadership repeatedly had to scramble to meet their payroll while the in-house bank SEB had plans to force the company into bankruptcy. Restructuring was successful and the Johnson Group reoriented towards wholesale and retailing, where they benefitted from new-born post-industrial society.[5]

Business Groups

Some dynasties have remained diversified in terms of the industries controlled. Since they are independent with respect to management operations, they are not conglomerates. Instead, they are business groups. The definition of a business group is a cluster of coordinated activities carried out by interlinked but legally independent enterprises. According to this, a business group should be a series of legally independent enterprises coordinated by an administrative entity or dynasty by means of capital expenditures, goods circulation, interlocking directorates, personal appointments and information sharing.

Business groups in the Nordic countries have emerged as a combination of cooperative capitalism, national economic goals and export orientation. The original formation back in the early twentieth century seems to have been a response to a situation where management costs and risks were considered too high to conduct industrial activities within a single, large enterprise. The emergence of business groups compensated for the institutional instability and the relative backwardness in Scandinavia at the time of the Industrial Revolution. They have used a strategy of diversification at the group level in order to share risks and reduce costs at the firm level. Thus, business groups do not exist only to solve the problem of market failure, but also to scale down internal management costs associated with a single, large enterprise.[6]

The largest business group in the Nordic countries is the Wallenberg sphere, in terms of market value of controlling interests and number of employees. Their largest holdings are Investor, Saab, Electrolux, SKF, StoraEnso, Atlas Copco, Ericsson, SEB, OMX, ABB, SAS and Astra Zeneca. Concerning line of business, there is a range from finance, engineering, defence and telecommunications to the aviation and pharmaceutical industries. There are also smaller holdings in emerging industries. The next largest business group has traditionally lacked family ownership, but the Lundberg family is slowly but surely accumulating influence through direct ownership of companies controlled by Handelsbanken's Foundations and the Industrivärden holding company. In 2016, Fredrik Lundberg was represented on the board of Industrivärden (chairman) and Handelsbanken. The holdings of Industrivärden consisted of SCA (paper and tissue), Volvo (lorries), Sandvik (mechanical tools), Ericsson (telecommunications), ICA (supermarkets), Skanska (building construction) and SSAB (steel). As with the Wallenberg Group, there is a wide range of lines of business.

In these two business groups, the holdings are listed companies and ownership is shared with others, although they might not be controlling owners. In three other Nordic business groups (Fred. Olsen, Ferd [the Andresen family] and Møller-Mærsk), most companies are unlisted subsidiaries. The Ferd conglomerate, established for the interests of the Andresen family in 2001, operates within industry and finance as well as real estate, while Fred. Olsen is engaged in transport, travel, energy and renewables, but also has minor ownership in other industries. A.P. Mærsk-Møller's activities are structured into several business segments, primarily within the transportation and the energy sectors, but the group also has long-term interests in shipyards, retail and banking.

Bonnier—Back to Basics

The story of the Bonnier Group exemplifies the difficulties that arise from long-term diversification when involvement and network capacity have to be transferred to a new generation of family members. The network of Lukas and Albert Bonnier Jr. had a clear hierarchy in the sense of fulfilling various functions within the group. In the media arena, contacts with editors and journalists were cultivated. It sought out individuals who could "wield the power of the pen," i.e., those able to assemble interesting stories and present information and facts in a way that appealed to the public. Transfer of the media network did not cause major problems when succession within the dynasty required the replacement of Lukas and Albert Jr. Younger family members and other executives had been trained and become experienced in the family's core activities over a long period. The extended family also had a distinct general interest in the media activities an interest based on their position and recognition in book publishing and newspaper production.

The entry into the industrial sector that had occurred during the 1950s to 1970s, with the purchase of firms in mechanical engineering, furniture production and the paper industry, however, became problematical. Here, the network was more compact and no family member in the generation after Albert Bonnier Jr. wanted, or was capable of, taking over responsibility for administration of these firms. The fact that several of them were struggling with red figures made them even less attractive. Since the competence and work motivation of the family were in the media arena, the interests developed by Albert Bonnier Jr. were sold after his death. The Bonnier dynasty returned to its core activities, following the principal of doing what you know and understand best.[7]

The sixth generation took up the gauntlet more easily when it came to the media, given that skills and motivation were still so salient in that area. At that point, family members and other employees had long since absorbed the lessons of fealty to the core business. Their general interest in media was a natural outgrowth of the status and recognition that the publication of books and periodicals that won for them in Sweden. The weight of history—the historical anchor—continued to draw the Bonnier dynasty to the Nordic media market.

The U-Turn of Lego

Kjeld Kirk, who led the third generation of Lego owners, advocated for ambitious 15% annual sales growth. His father Godtfred, chairman of the board, was far from enamoured of such new-fangled ideas, prioritising consolidation and low indebtedness: "My best advice to Kjeld is therefore: let's continue to focus all our efforts on the idea of Lego—but obviously without being blinkered. Explore in depth, and the ideas will come."[8] After Kjeld took over in 1979, he felt it his duty to apply the dictates of diversified growth that he had picked up during his university studies in Denmark and Switzerland. His adventures imperilled the future of the business, while Godtfried devoted himself KIRKBI, the family investment firm, until his death in 1995.

Among the speculative projects that devoured the most resources were video and computer software in a pitch for Hollywood and the youth market. Fearful that everyday plastic blocks stood no chance against the Goliath of digital technology, he strayed farther and farther from the bedrock of the business. But his strategic choices were met with scepticism, and his distribution of high dividends to himself and purchases of three jet planes earned him the reputation of a megalomaniac. Once losses mounted and there was no more money to throw away, the only way to survive was to sell the Legoland parks. By the time new millennium rolled around, Kjeld had no credibility left with the board, which chose Jørgen Vig Knudstorp (the first outsider in the company's history) to right the ship. He quickly consolidated operations, restoring profitability and the core business.[9]

In terms of leadership, father and son were as different as night and day. Godtfred was a species of autodidact as an entrepreneur, whereas Kjeld proceeded from the theoretical knowledge he had acquired abroad. No doubt the company was far from the same congenial affair when he took the rudder in 1979 as when his father had earned such esteem for his personal touch with employees, suppliers and customers. But his tenure has been widely panned as too commercial and programmatic, lacking the intuitive flair that ongoing modernization of the brand demanded.[10] The U-turn his successor took bore out his father's prophecy that the business would thrive only when it stuck to what it knew best. The debacle at the management level notwithstanding, the family maintained its controlling interest in the group and passed the chairmanship on to fourth generation scion Thomas Kirk Kristiansen in 2016.

Too Much Tradition Kills

The history of Nordic dynasties suggests that excessive regard to tradition can be devastating. Conservatism is part of the historical roots and can bind the operations in a negative way at a time where the push of the market moves competitors forward. The behaviour can take the form of uncritical acceptance of the strategies of earlier generations or rejecting new initiatives, as obstacles to new ideas and renewal. In the long run, this might result in less sentimental (non-family owned) companies developing more rapidly. History is full of mature and emerging dynasties that have lost their role in the economy just because they have stuck to what they already know. They have been too conservative in times when the circumstances called for renewal and creative destruction.

Many of these expired large family businesses share the misfortune of belonging to industries that have lost competitiveness due to increased internationalization (shipbuilding, shipping, textiles). In other cases, the family has lacked key competence and the financial strength required to maintain ownership control. Becoming a majority owner has not been sufficient to guarantee survival. Two critical factors have been the family's inability to maintain enough liquidity and recruit qualified and motivated co-workers. When facing a recession, the family has not been able to make long-term investment decision to challenge or compensate for less favourable markets.

The case of Saléninvest, a highly diversified family group with large investments in ship owning in the 1970s, is a good example of the fact that too much tradition can be devastating.[11] The group was listed on the stock exchange but with controlling blocks of shares held by family members and non-family managers. In this case, de-diversification came too late, resulting in the firm's bankruptcy in 1984. The fact that the company had even survived so long was partly the result of new sources of credit and partly of assets that could be sold. Most board members and top managers of Saléninvest had a strong aversion to abandoning the firm's core function, preferring to sell off profitable activities that belonged to previous diversification. During the second half of the 1970s, a share portfolio whose return stabilized the liquidity variability that characterized the ship owning branch had been accumulated. There were also other profitable activities in the areas of real estate, energy, trading and import of cars (Toyota). Without the revenue from these operations, Saléninvest would have already been insolvent in the 1970s.

When the lack of liquidity became acute, however, none of these profitable activities was retained. The family of Salén saw itself as ship-owners with their key competence in the area of shipping, and the problems in this industry were deemed to be temporary. Exaggerated regard for the strategies followed by earlier generations resulted in leadership refusing to abandon the unprofitable shipping business. This conservative tendency unquestionably impeded Saléninvest's renewal options. To a certain extent, the strategic inertia was the result of a commission agreement that made the capital in the parent company subject to centrally planned investment decisions. Sale of the tankers would automatically worsen the security situation for the banks that provided credit. Because they had not lent money to the tanker fleet specifically, but to the concern as a whole, they opposed sales that would result in losses.[12]

In the Wrong Industry at the Wrong Time

The Salén case echoes the development of the Italian family group Falck, whose strategy was to stick to tradition—once a steel company, always a steel-company—and that diversified too late and consequently lost altitude in the Italian economy.[13] But there are also similarities to other family-based shipping firms in Scandinavia that were hit by the slump. In the 1960s, Broström was the largest employer in Gothenburg, with 18,000 employees.[14] The fleet consisted of 81 large vessels, equal to one-third of the merchant fleet in Sweden. When they were hit by the structural crisis in the 1970s, they were unable to solve their problems. The identity of being a shipping family was simply too strong. During the recession, they continued to order new ships (roll-on, roll-off), although the group was bleeding financially. In 1984, most of the assets had been sold out and the rubbles of the former proud dynasty were taken over in 2008 by A.P. Møller-Mærsk, which shut down the office in Gothenburg four years later. The three-generation story of Broström not only confirms the Buddenbrooks syndrome but also illustrates the negative side of historical roots once strong external forces set in.

Since every shipping company was hit by the 1970s crisis, the failure of many family-based shipping firms was externally determined. However, not everyone had to give up. There are at least two reasons Møller-Mærsk and Fred. Olson survived and not Broström and Saléninvest: one institutional and one strategic. The left-wing parties and labour unions in Sweden strongly opposed low-flag carriers, while Denmark and Norway established an international register to survive in competition with aggressive, low-cost countries. Swedish ship-owners accused the government of making it impossible to compete internationally, and approximately 160 Swedish ships were sold abroad between 1975 and 1979. In contrast to Denmark and Norway, Swedish national institutions were not optimal.[15]

Second, Danish and Norwegian firms did not sell off non-core holdings. Instead, they used previous diversification into counter-cyclical sectors to compensate for the huge losses in the shipping market. Møller-Mærsk had a diversified portfolio, including oil and gas on the North Sea, chemical industry, steel, finance and aviation. Likewise, Fred. Olsen continues to benefit from long-term holdings in the mechanical industry, airline transport and energy sectors. Most of these industries were counter-cyclical to the shipping market with its strong ups and downs. In hindsight, the strategic choices of the largest Danish and Norwegian shipping firms were superior to these two Swedish competitors. As an example, when Saléninvest ordered new tankers in the early 1970s, Fred. Olsen sold its tanker interests and did not re-enter until the mid-1980s when the slump was over.[16] At that point, the fleets of Broström and Salén invest had disappeared from the oceans due to insurmountable liquidity problems.

To conclude, in the volatile shipping market, it was harmful to leave the track of diversification. The business concept of ordering new ships and buying secondary ones during slumps in order to stay prepared for an improvement in the market became a useless strategy during the long recession. Therefore, groups that identity themselves entirely as shipping firms lost while those that carried on as diversified ones, like Mærsk Mc-Kinney or Olsen, or carved out a niche market, as Olsson, stayed in business.

Continuity and Discontinuity with Historical Roots

The reason most dynasties have held on to the same line of business is that they develop knowledge of products, customers and suppliers that is unique. This critical knowledge is difficult for others to copy and compete with, especially non-family businesses, since they change ownership and management more often.[17] In family businesses, this knowledge is transferred and deepened from one generation to the next and becomes part of the corporate culture: an impregnable fortress of competencies impossible for non-family businesses to imitate.

This provides incentive for sticking to what you already know in terms of products and customers, to continue in the same type of business as previous generations. On the other hand, continuous industrial renewal can also be a tradition to hold on to, where every new generation has the potential to bring ambitious entrepreneurship into the family business. There are many examples of kick-starts after the young generation has taken over the controls.

There seem to be three categories of structural development among dynasties. For many dynasties, it has been enough to maintain the original break with industry logic. Based on the innovation of the founder or someone in a later generation, the business has focused on expanding the market for the products worldwide. Both mature and emerging dynasties are found in this category. Others have kept the core activity but also entered related sector in the pursuit of profitable new markets. They have benefited from vertical and horizontal integration but also integrated industries that have been counter-cyclical to the core holdings.

The dynasties in the third category have been increasingly dependent on emerging new industries, leaving their activities in forestry, engineering, pulp and paper and other traditional industries behind them. The commitments have turned to industries such as energy, ICT and retail.

These three different ways suggest there has not been any general recipe for staying alive as a dynasty. The timing of diversification and de-diversification has been crucial for the choices made. In general, too much consideration to the glorious days in the past has been devastating for strategic choices. Thus, the best recipe for survival seems to be deep passion for the business in a family capable of critically reflecting on its historical achievements, eager to find alternative routes for the journey ahead.

The need for the captains of family businesses to navigate the straits of technology, consumer habits, institutions, political ground rules and the market forms the backdrop to a pageant of both continuity and quantum leaps. Paradoxically perhaps, long-term survival may rely on both phenomena. Whereas continuity is vital to creating value under stable organizational and operative conditions, casting aside inefficient structures and counterproductive incentives is the life blood of all organic entities. Death and resurrection are two sides of the same coin. The dynamism of dynasties has frequently returned after a reassessment that led to abandonment of their most sacred assumptions.

This overview of the forces that have driven structural change for several dynasties leaves room for three observations. Number one: holding onto the original industry, products and services is often a successful survival strategy. The same may be said of the organizational and institutional scaffolding (historical anchor), particularly when it comes to retaining control of a shifting market. Running a business might face entirely different challenges in the age of information than in an agricultural economy (the predominant employer until after World War II), but family businesses have generally done best by standing their ground. If the industry where all things started has remained profitable, continuity tends to emerge victorious.

Number two: while many companies ruled by dynasties rode the wave of restructuring from the United States, continuity in relation to the core business was rarely sacrificed. Nevertheless, diversified structures certainly existed before a European version emerged in the shadow of the multi-industry American corporations that flowered after World War II. Anxious to spread risks and attract the customers of the future, family businesses that adopted the new philosophy began exploring industries far from the time-worn path.

The Stenbecks abandoned their core business without a trace left behind. The Bonniers, Johnsons and Kristiansens, on the other hand, came crawling back to the security of the past (historical anchor) after having suffered crushing losses. In retrospect, some of the projects that family members embarked on when liquidity was favourable were little more than shady speculation. What was at stake was not simply a controlling interest, but an entire fortune. The Saléns learned the hard way that a flight back to the core business after a period of heavy diversification may not suffice to ensure long-term survival. The challenges facing the Swedish shipping industry in the 1970s and beyond were much too imposing.

Number three: constant renewal is also a form or state of continuity. To guarantee capabilities for being flexible and ready to adapt to the changing internal and external environment. Without compromising on value creation in older industries, the Ehrnrooths and Wallenbergs set their sights on new businesses, some of which skyrocketed after being listed. The Stenbecks enjoyed similar success after throwing the legacy of industrial society under the bus in favour of key industries at the power centres of the digital age. In other words, dynasties have taken many different roads to the same goal. The range of choices available to the family when encountering the winds of renewal stem from their unique ability to combine long-term committed ownership with the relationships, networking skills and value-oriented philosophies.

Notes

1. Sjögren (2012), p. 28.
2. Sjögren (2012), pp. 28–31.
3. Sjögren (2012), pp. 21–31.
4. Ericson (1982) and De Geer (1998), pp. 417–519.
5. De Geer (1998), pp. 552–4 and Ericson (2007).
6. Zhang et al. (2016).
7. Larsson (2006), pp. 348–9 and Larsson (2001), pp. 147–51.
8. Lunde (2012), p. 33.

 9. Cortzen (1996), pp. 272–4 and Lunde (2012), pp. 112–205.
10. Lunde (2012), pp. 268; 270.
11. Sjögren (1999).
12. Sjögren (1999).
13. James (2006).
14. Mattsson (1984).
15. Taudal Poulsen et al. (2012), pp. 106–7.
16. Ellemose (2004) and Gulbrandsen and Lange (2009), pp. 184–9.
17. Nordqvist (2016), p. 11.

5 Values and Credos

Dynasties pass down commandments, slogans and unwritten laws. Jan Stenbeck compared them to the tablets that Moses received from God on Mount Sinai. Not to be outdone by his father Hugo, he added a few of his own. Biographies of the family mention those that flourished the most. English was the official language of the group and so were the commandments. Unsurprisingly, the first commandment was "thou shalt obey." As much as employees were baptized in the virtues of entrepreneurship and high-risk projects, the empire itself was patriarchal and hierarchical and nobody ever doubted who was in charge. Another commandment was "thou shalt not be naive." Translated into business speak, make every business decision realistically and choose cynicism over optimism when the two collide. The commandment "always hire the best" warned against the folly of prestige worship and nepotism in all its manifestations. The bottom line was to eliminate conflicting loyalties.[1]

The commandment "thou shalt maintain control" addressed the responsibilities inherent to being a senior executive. A less biblical sounding commandment dictated that at least two Stenbeck representatives attend any negotiating session. "Do it the way we always have" stressed the importance of taking the path of least resistance. If you absolutely had to reinvent the wheel for a project to succeed, so be it—the ends always justified the means. Stenbeck's version of the seventh commandment was, "Thou shalt not sleep with thy customers, suppliers or employees." Unholy alliances and unbusiness-like decisions were again the bugaboo. Stenbeck appointed only men to top positions, and dependence on a woman in the organisation carried in his mind the risk of favours, aristocratic privileges and personal considerations. He went so far as to fire two executives who flouted the commandment and pushed another one out the door.[2]

He couldn't have chosen a more effective way to convey the impression of a Machiavellian culture where he played the role of a feared rather than a beloved prince over a clan under the whip of performance and results. As a Gordon Gekko in a Swedish suit, Stenbeck counted both friends and enemies among his colleagues. Many who ultimately left his world said something to the effect that he was a brilliant and talented man who finally wore them out. His revolving door of managers did not always leave by their own choice. His language was harsh, often seasoned with obscenities and sexual innuendos. His typical instructions were "Shut up" and "Do what I say."[3]

Servant of the People—Kamprad's Will

While Ingvar Kamprad was a different kind of leader than Stenbeck, a general in the spirit of enlightened capitalism is capable of a commandment or two, if more gentle. His panoply of insights as an entrepreneur and merchant span the second half of the twentieth century. His detailed, nine-point *A Furniture Dealer's Testament* contains several dictates that are particular to his industry and others that are of general human interest. The first one addresses the essence of the Ikea identity and brand—the importance of choosing the right assortment. The fundamental principle is to offer a broad range of attractive, functional merchandise at prices such that as many people as possible can afford them ("creating a better life for the masses").[4]

Dictate no. 2 stresses the team spirit and participatory atmosphere that maintain the loyalty of customers, suppliers and employees alike. Just like in football where the coach is responsible for bringing the best out of each player, who must keep their eye on what they can contribute to the team as a whole. "Never underestimate the value of good Samaritans," Kamprad said,

> the simple, quiet and unpretentious people who are always ready to lend a helping hand. They do their duty without any fanfare. They understand the concept of responsibility but don't want to be limited by it. Sharing and being there for others are the ultimate secrets of their ability to contribute.[5]

Dictate no. 3, "profits allow us to grow," also reflect a sense of obligation, as well as traditional southern Swedish cost consciousness. The secret is to husband your resources better than anyone else by means of efficient product development, thrifty purchasing and overall frugality. No stranger to flea markets, he applied his observations to Ikea's pricing policies. According to Kamprad's fourth dictate, "Wasting valuable resources is a mortal sin." For him, Ikea was a sterling example of the potential for achieving great things with limited means. These last two dictates both target long-term value.[6]

Next comes the entreaty to strive for simplicity and shun bureaucracy, the evil monster of complexity and paralysis. Simple procedures bring power and clarity, while humble conduct promotes team spirit. Even when choosing hotel rooms, making travel plans and forming consumer habits, restraint and modesty are always to be preferred. Kamprad offered himself as a role model, always flying economy class. Senior executives were expected to take the bus or metro rather than a taxi or rental car, not only for the sake of moderation but to maintain the common touch. "Simple procedures, simple conduct, simple lives. Price isn't the only reason for avoiding luxurious hotels. We don't need flashy cars or status symbols. We empower ourselves."[7] The approach is said to have cut costs for air travel, hotels and rental cars by 20%–40%, not to mention greater exposure to potential customers.[8]

The next dictate is based on the concept of thinking outside the box and steering clear of the beaten path. Asking why is the first step towards building a creative, flexible organization. The seventh dictate stresses the importance of focusing on one thing at a time. Achieving success and breakthroughs in strategic markets requires a concerted effort every once in a while.[9]

The eighth dictate is "Responsibility brings benefits." According to Kamprad,

> Wisdom and independence are the keys to effective decision making. Mistakes are part of the process. Trying to prove that you are always right leads only to mediocrity. Strength is forward-looking. Optimists always win. They are a source of pleasure to both themselves and others.[10]

In other words, employees have both the right and obligation to make informed decisions.

Not content to rest on his laurels, Kamprad said that a lot remain to be done. "The future is ours. Past is prelude" is the final dictate. The sense of completion, he argued, can be soporific and experience may hold back progress—the joy of experimentation is the foundation of growth and improvement. Kamprad also presented his advice as a list accompanied by quotes. A few examples might provide the basis for setting targets and spurring growth among all entrepreneurs.[11]

- Come up with a business concept.
- Cut your dreams down to reality—remember Icarus.
- Don't be afraid to run your idea by the most honest and perceptive person you know—and listen closely to what they have to say.
- Expect to give more of your life to the company than you would have thought possible.
- Analyze your faults and look yourself squarely in the eye.
- Surround yourself with people who can make up for your weaknesses.
- Buy cheap and sell even cheaper than your competitors.
- Be tenacious and diligent but don't forget to make a decision.
- Avoid the trap of dependence, be thrifty.

- Start with the kitchen table, buy an expensive desk later on (maybe).
- Don't drop the ball after making a decision.
- Get out of your ivory tower—the warehouse will tell you a lot more than statistics on paper.
- Find an office within walking distance of the plant.
- Remember that your country needs you more than ever.
- Keep in mind that honesty is the best policy and that win-win situations are always best.

Cost consciousness, enthusiasm, simplicity and togetherness form the essence of Kamprad's message. The lowest common denominator and core value is humility, as testified to by many outsiders who have been exposed to the Ikea corporate culture. Combined with determination and a dash of risk-taking, growth may assume the kinds of proportions that the familiar international brand has exhibited.

The fundamental business concept permeates everything that the company does. Employees are expected to think about the success of the enterprise and brand at each step of the way. What passes for a uniform is an open-collar sport shirt, casual jeans and occasional sweater. A total of 155,000 workers in 43 countries on every continent have something to share. The province of Småland has never been larger. As Kamprad put it, "China is a rerun of the world I grew up in."[12]

Renewal and the National Interest—the Wallenbergs

According to Kamprad's final dictate, the greatest satisfaction is derived from the journey rather than the destination. Similarly, the Wallenberg's first rule for successful corporate governance is, "The only tradition worth cherishing is the need for continual renewal." Entrepreneurship that never relents is the catalyst that fuels both individual companies and the economy as a whole. The rules have taken shape for five generations since André Oscar Wallenberg founded SEB at the advent of Swedish liberalism and industrialism.[13]

It goes without saying that the dynasty's most important principle is a sense of responsibility for the Wallenberg companies and their controlling interests. Principle number two is "Esse non videri," interpreted by historians of the family to means "Be without appearing to be" so as to avoid a suggestion of Mafia-like behaviour. Growth and performance trump celebrity, renown and personal pleasure. The third principle concerns the role of dynasties in political deals and international private sector organizations. The family shall promote the interests of Sweden as a nation, as well as the formation and nurturance of effective global institutions.

The fourth principle is the fruit of the bitter experience of major recessions. Financial prudence and the ability to consolidate with an eye on long-term success and survival are crucial. Seeing the big picture and having an owner with enduring financial strength represent the best guarantee that value can be created on an ongoing basis. These lessons stemmed from a liquidity crisis in 1878 when the family's commercial venture might have come crashing down had not the government thrown it a lifeline. The dynastic interests faced a similar challenge in the wake of continual expansion and reconstruction during the years leading up to World War II. Such success has bred an unwavering faith that industrial and financial expertise add value as long as caution and perseverance are brought to bear.

A kindred principle is, "Long-time committed ownership does not necessary require wholly owned companies except during transitional stages." Such a phase may be a crisis during which the principal share-holders need full control to carry out their reconstruction effort. The purpose of soliciting other owners in normal times is not only to reduce the commitment of the controlling interest but exert greater pressure on executive management. For example, the corporate governance of Ericsson has taken such an approach, with two equally strong controlling owners (Investor and Industrivärden).[14]

According to the next Wallenberg dictate, "Every company should focus on exports and international competitiveness to offset the limitations that are inherent to a small domestic market." The products developed during the Industrial Revolution blazed the trail for new technologies, as well as prosperity and big earnings in the Swedish agricultural economy. Following a close examination of innovations in the United States and elsewhere, entrepreneurs would seek public and private venture capital to plunge ahead. Once the industrial economy had taken over, product development continued to keep one eye on exports, adding new innovations in the burgeoning pharmaceutical, aviation and automotive industries, just to name a few.

The credo of the Wallenberg dynasty reflects just how integral it has been to the evolution of the Swedish private sector over the past century and a half. The long parade of industrial and financial crises has left an indelible impression. The principles are also an outgrowth of the political role that members of the family have played (Knut Agathon Wallenberg was the Minister of Foreign Affairs in 1914–1917), as well as their participation in international negotiations during the world wars. Other dynasties have cultivated similar patriotic notions, if not the same kind of political status.

One piece of advice that Kamprad proffered was, "Remember that your country needs you more than ever." According to the Swedish Institute, Ikea has done more than all government agencies combined to put the country on the map as an example of self-reliance and elegant simplicity.[15] Not bad considering that the holding company is in the Netherlands, the head office in Denmark, production in Poland and the foundation in Lichtenstein. Be that as it may, an individual dynasty in a small, open economy clearly has the potential to outdo the state's propaganda machine at a time when the welfare state is but a distant memory.

After decades of successful entrepreneurship, families can boast of the exports, employment opportunities and affluence they have generated in the national interest. And the mature ones can look back on the relief they have provided in healing the wounds of the world wars. Nor has loyalty to country sagged under the weight of globalization and relocation of production abroad. Founder Peter Mærsk articulated it this way in 1899: "If we are to withstand the competition with other countries, there is a need for thoughtfulness, proficiency and diligence, both among those who work with their heads and among those who work with their hands."[16] The emphasis here is obviously on the marriage of theory and practice. At the age of 80, his son A.P. Møller looked back on his life: "Since I was very young, it has been an aim in my life to accomplish something in Denmark and earn funding abroad to increase the general opportunities in Denmark."[17] Not surprisingly, Mærsk Mc-Kinney Møller inherited the conviction of his forbears that exalting and working on behalf of Denmark was a virtue in itself.

Resolute Leadership

The Wallenberg dynasty has two maxims about the role of the individual in an organization. Marcus Wallenberg Sr. coined the first one: "First the captain, then the ship." He demanded a corporate culture that would foster leadership based on verve, creativity, consistency and an eye for constructive acquisitions. In other words, no company is so bad that it can't be rescued by a smart CEO or so good that it can't be destroyed by a dumb one. The other maxim is more pragmatic than theoretical: "Technologically savvy executives are the key to success for most of our holdings." The company turned all of its attention to Asea/ABB, Atlas Copco and other manufacturers at which only engineers with economic expertise were considered for the highest post. The plethora of holdings ensures a pool of capable employees who can be rotated among various positions and projects. Promising young recruits receive more and more responsibilities as managers at the ever-expanding array of companies.[18]

"Preserving the good reputation of the Wallenberg brand" breathes confidence in having climbed to the top ranks of Swedish and international business. A name associated with status and prestige is a powerful symbolic asset when accumulating relational capital. Knut Wallenberg, who had no children himself, waxed lyrical when his nephew Jacob turned 30 in 1922.

> Restraint is the mother of success. Countless are those who have fallen because they lacked the will or wisdom to show restraint. Never look down on others. You do so at your own risk. And above

all, remember your grandfather's edict to future generations: Cherish and treasure our name.[19]

The legendary Mærsk Mc-Kinney Møller never tired of the subject. "Our name is our greatest obligation, and I remind all the employees to nurture it. It was created on the initiative of Mr A.P. Møller, back in 1904. The world at large recognizes it and trusts it. It must not be squashed."[20] Given that Mærsk and the brand were indistinguishable, he instinctively included employees in the enterprise.

Because the Bonniers, Mærsk Mc-Kinneys and Wallenbergs are fixtures in the economic and cultural elite of Nordic history, the name itself gives them a leg up in a number of different venues. The other side of the coin is that members of the family may have trouble obtaining ordinary jobs on the suspicion that they are pariahs for some reason or are only looking for a temporary pastime. The founder's name is both an obligation and limitation for subsequent generations.

The network of executives with bonds of loyalty to the Wallenbergs must accept that they will be pigeonholed throughout their careers. Apart from competitive pay scales, recruitment of non-family members to absorb the corporate and dynastic culture is a tool for continual renewal. Ambitious, well-educated young people certainly take the prestigious name of their prospective employer into consideration. Working for the Wallenbergs, Herlins, Kamprads, Paasikivis and Mærsk Mc-Kinneys, for example, lends a dimension absent from an ordinary company. Which isn't to say that the gravitational pull retains its strength if kinship appears to take precedence over ability within the organization. When Johan Stenebo broke with Kamprad and Ikea, he may have been reacting to that kind of nepotism. After 20 years of executive positions and without losing his admiration for Kamprad, he found himself in an identity crisis that seriously tarnished the dynastic aura. Not only that, but whether Kamprad's sons had what it took to carry the baton further was in serious question. According to Stenebo,

> Ikea has always surrounded itself with an impenetrable facade. The media and general public have been fed a jumble of truths, half-truths and lies: stories of success, unconventional solutions, an indefatigable entrepreneur who practices the austerity he preaches, the principled, socially and environmentally aware company, the well-heeled sons who walk humbly in their father's footsteps.[21]

Here Stenebo wrests the tablet of commandments out of Kamprad's hands and questions Ikea's image of itself. His own description may be heavily subjective and tinged by vengeance, but it is a valuable tool in understanding the impact of firm leadership on succession in a large, successful family business. It also provides a little perspective on Kamprad's tendency to melancholy, to wit, "Don't call me the best. I've made more mistakes than you can count."[22]

The critique that Ruben Rausing and his charismatic leadership style attracted is pertinent here as well. He has been portrayed as having omnipotent pretentions, capable of anything that you can imagine when it came to innovation and benefactor. At his most delusional, he dreamed of winning the Nobel Prize in Medicine. Fooled by the same magnificent phantasms, he promised market triumphs that his employees could see right through while insulting them to their faces. Nevertheless, he was an unfailing judge of ability and eventually scored huge sales gains. According to his biographer, he passed the myth of infallibility down to his sons, who turned it into a dogma. If your name was Rausing, your decisions were per definition beyond reproach.[23]

Spotlight on Customers—the Perssons, Rausings and Kann Rasmussens

Erling Persson, the founder of H&M, also articulated rules of thumb and pearls of wisdom. They are concrete, down-to-earth and indelibly stamped with the logic and assumptions of the clothing industry. One idée fixe is that unsold merchandise is both a major expense and an unnecessary risk. Balance sheets, he also emphasizes, must be strong to fend off the many challenges that ultimately come along. Bordering on business strategy, many of these concepts address the best way to structure marketing and sales in the service of optimum performance. The capacity to negotiate, compromise with and read others was also enshrined in the family canon. The entrepreneurial spirit and the concept of controlled imagination were Persson's recipe for finding employees who could exhibit constructive creativity and the ability to implement effective solutions.[24] The family were urged to take advantage of its networking potential, cultivate relational capital and welcome people who were visionary but not utopian in their outlooks.

Both Erling and Stefan Persson have clearly demonstrated that such a philosophy can generate extraordinary profitability and value. Maintaining close, supportive relationships with customers is inherent to everything they do. Instead of asking directly as is typically the case, they have been willing to try out the innovative approaches that they truly believe in. The habit of relying more on fashion they have designed in-house is a reflection of the same daring spirit. Much of the practical ideology that the Perssons espouse proceeds from simplicity, disdain for bureaucracy and rejection of academic cleverness.

They could easily endorse Kamprad's exhortation to "market our most important products as typical of the company in Scandinavia and typical of Sweden abroad." Ikea's surveys have shown that Sweden is more of a winning brand than Scandinavia.[25]

The Perssons are also reminiscent of the Tetra Pak experience that financial reward is the result of innovations that improve living standards for the general public more than for the 1%. Rausing was a visionary who was constantly on the lookout for new technologies, distribution systems and organizational structures. His rare networking abilities, charisma and inquisitiveness attracted imaginative, inventive people who could apply their ideas under his protective tutelage. The pragmatic beliefs were fuelled by the desire to make dreams come true, make money and establish a dynasty. His courage and willingness to assume risks paid off handsomely, while his patriarchal leadership was a potpourri of magnificence and pettiness, generosity and stinginess, genius and conceit.[26]

Long before the ground-breaking tetrahedron, Rausing articulated business tenets that formed a scaffolding for his dynasty and lifetime achievements. In brief, ideas should govern everything that an enterprise does. He wrote as early as 1930,

> A company constantly builds on the foundation of its business concept and principles. That's where they acquire their focus, impetus, spirit and life force. Its buildings, machinery, projects and other physical manifestations are shaped from the guidelines that the original ideas spawn. Employees live and breathe in that rarefied atmosphere. The idea that pervades Åkerlund & Rausing is very simple: streamlining the distribution of goods by virtue of packaging that is convenient for consumers and efficient for shippers.[27]

Like many entrepreneurs of the time, Villum Kann Rasmussen was influenced by the precepts of administration and executive leadership promulgated by Henri Fayol. Human resources were the core of any organization, and Fayol stressed the importance of involving everyone in the company's growth, cultivating team spirit and encouraging initiative. The ethical principles of management were also vital to disseminating a sense of responsibility, discipline, duty and consensus. Proceeding from such notions, Kann Rasmussen formulated a worldview of his own:

> A model enterprise is a commercial enterprise that is engaged in socially beneficial production and is managed in such a way that it treats its customers and suppliers, its employees of all categories and its shareholders better than most other commercial enterprises in the country.[28]

The objective was ambitious to say the least. Product development was to be the outgrowth of fruitful relationships and an environment that inspired extraordinary effort. Customers would not be won by undercutting the market but by offering durable, high-quality products. The company was broken down into small divisions, each of which was to operate in the black to attain Kann Rasmussen's goals of independence from internal external financing. The views that he penned and that are still very much the norm at VKR Holding largely reflects the stakeholder, as opposed to the shareholder value model.[29]

The Devil Is in the Details

The Mærsk credo stems from the company's formation but was not articulated in writing until A.P. Møller took the plunge in 1946: "My old maxim, that no loss that can be avoided with due care should strike us, must be a watchword that pervades the organization."[30] The words in Danish to remember are *rettidig omhu*, suggesting that shortcuts are to be eschewed in favour of structure and planning. Each and every employee is responsible for helping ensure that goods and services are provided as reliably and qualitatively as possible. The need for vigilance, foresight and preparation for mistakes is also part of that injunction. The trenchant expression has almost become a household word in Denmark. A translation to modern management jargon might be due diligence.

Mærsk Mc-Kinney Møller was quick to discover that manna does not fall from heaven but that intelligence and long hours at the office eventually do the trick. Duty, watchfulness, loyalty and discipline informed his approach to running a company. His father taught him that "what's worth doing is worth doing well."[31] Both personal conduct and attire were embodiments of such virtues. Men were expected to wear a suit, and women a dress. A strict dress code would demonstrate respect and seriousness both within the organization and when people from other cultures and countries paid a visit.

The philosophy acquired additional gravitas after Møller summoned executives to his home in 2003 for the launch of a "value process." He introduced five fundamental principles for the organizational and corporate culture: *rettidig omhu*, humility, integrity, brand and employee commitment. Each employee was to be challenged and prepared to promote ongoing improvements, while the organization as a whole was to exhibit transparency and responsibility at each step along the way. And the name was to carry its own weight—outsiders had the right to anticipate a common-sense, business-like approach whenever someone from A.P. Møller-Mærsk made an appearance. Each division was charged with ensuring that its employees lived up to the five principles. That is as true now as it ever was. Møller put it in a nutshell during his last interview: "The basic principle is that people should be able to rely on us. The authorities can rely on us, our employees can rely on us, and our business contacts can rely on us. We keep our promises."[32]

When Ole and Godtfred Kirk Kristiansen laid the cornerstone for one of the most dynamic brands ever at Lego, attention to detail was again at centre stage. An old saying, "the best is not too good," was used to hammer home the virtues of quality, renewal and disciplined imagination. The concepts have made an indelible impression on the organization. The first time Godtfred heard the expression from Ole, he went out to the shed, carved the words in a wooden plaque and hung it on the wall. The slogan appeared in thousands of ads and steered the ship of the entire organization.[33]

In a eulogy at his father's funeral, Kjeld Kirk Kristiansen referred to it as the company's guiding star. The philosophy urged everyone to think one step ahead and serve as an example of progress: "Never be completely satisfied, because if you are you will stop creating, my father often said."[34] Renewal makes the world go around. Stagnation is another word for decline. Among additional principles that the family passed down to future generations were "responsibility, honesty, modesty, conscientiousness, respect and concern for the individual."[35] Though not a direct influence, Weber's Protestant Ethic clearly played a role. Corporate governance was animated by the spirit of capitalism that had fired Western economies since the Industrial Revolution: diligence, frugality, simplicity, unpretentiousness and other middle-class virtues.

Ole Kirk promulgated the faith that skill, industry and honesty were the source of all great accomplishments. Until the early 1960s, workers (the half who agreed to participate) began each day with a 10-minute group prayer session.[36] His grandson Kjeld was still carrying on the tradition, at least within the family.[37] According to an interview in 1990, Godtfred emphasized that he placed intangible virtues above pecuniary considerations.

> Money as such does not interest me—it's merely a means of enabling things to happen and succeed. However, you obviously have to make sure you have a bit more than you need. For me, money has always come fourth: number 1 is the idea (the right one), number 2 is quality, number 3 is capable and qualified staff—and then comes money, the necessary capital as a result.[38]

These principles led the way, as a simple wood toyshop became a leading Danish corporation in a matter of 30 years. The events were very similar to the Ikea story during the same period. Without the help of higher education, management theory or foreign language skills, both entrepreneurs inspired those around them to overcome obstacles, exhibit respect and exploit the ripple effects of creativity and cost-effectiveness. In Godtfred's words, "What would I, poor man, have done without being open to thoughts and ideas from the many employees in Denmark and abroad?"[39]

Antonia Ax:son Johnson spoke in the same vein: "A good company assumes responsibility for goods, services, employees, quality, durability, health and the satisfaction of demand." Her ethical approach was reinforced in the late 1980s when the company sagged under the weight of family feuds, too much delegation of authority and short-term thinking. She solicited objectivity and leadership that renounced avarice. "I don't think we fully understand the paradox of our times. A sense of perspective ensures success, appropriate distance and focused commitment. Without it, achievements blow away like leaves in the wind."[40]

As the sole potentate of an extraordinarily successful dynasty, she pursued a general code of conduct and principles. Her philosophy took aim at the excesses and limitations inherent to the short-sighted quest for profits. Her concept of the good embraced both the Golden Rule of Taoism ("Regard your neighbour's gain as your gain, and your neighbour's loss as your own loss"), as well as several of the Judaeo-Christian commandments.

Winning Strategies

A core feature of long-lived dynasties is the propagation of strategic philosophes that provide discipline and guidance for employees. This chapter has sketched the credos of the Johnsons, Kamprads, Kristiansens, Mærsk Mc-Kinneys, Perssons, Stenbecks and Wallenbergs.

Many of them clearly overlap, particularly when it comes to transparent, purposeful leadership, self-financing, strong balance sheets, organic growth, ground-breaking entrepreneurship and control of business processes. To a significant extent, the thinking is no different than that of most profit-making enterprises. In that sense, they are the building blocks of all market economies rather than the prodigies of familial interests. Nevertheless, each dynasty gives rise to its own unique way of looking at things as a reflection of the industry in which it finds itself. Some of them hone in on efficient management of the accumulated wealth and holdings by a foundation. Others concentrate on perpetuating the dynasty by ensuring that employees and family members assume and grow into their proper roles.

Between the lines is the expectation that all conduct will further the interests conveyed by the patriarch or matriarch. These ideologies are particularly relevant during formative stages and periods of succession, not to mention unusual pressure from financial markets and policymakers. And finally there are belief systems that serve as a moral compass when the head of the family deals with others. The goal is a mutual feeling of trust with employees, customers, suppliers, lenders, policymakers and anyone whose good graces are important.

The entire attitude strongly resembles Weber's Protestant Ethic (people serve God by committing themselves fully to their profession). Work is a calling (*Ora et laboro*). Intimately connected with the work ethic was the demand for a puritanical kind of moderation bordering on asceticism. The default purpose of income is to save while awaiting reinvestment in business and career. Lending is also permitted as an expression of trust, particularly among those who live god-fearing lives. Not coincidentally, the word credit comes from the Latin *credere*, meaning "to trust" or to have faith that the other person will hold up their end of the bargain. The values of the founder as embodied by future generations, reflect these features of the spirit of capitalism, as opposed to professional and provide debt, profligacy and debauchery.

Notes

1. Andersson (2000), p. 343.
2. Andersson (2000), pp. 344–7.
3. Björk (2006), pp. 271–2.
4. See Björk (1998), p. 13.
5. Torekull (2006), pp. 336–9.
6. Torekull (2006), pp. 336–9.
7. Torekull (2011), p. 111.
8. Björk (1998), pp. 163–4.
9. Björk (1998), pp. 63–4.
10. Torekull (2006), pp. 336–9.
11. Torekull (2011), pp. 64–5.
12. Björk (1998), p. 171 and Torekull (2011), p. 18 (citation).
13. Carlsson (2001).
14. Carlsson (2001). See also Economist (2016).
15. Kristoffersson (2014), p. 79.
16. Ellemose (2004), p. 385.
17. Ellemose (2004), p. 371.
18. Carlsson (2001).
19. Olsson (2006), p. 436.
20. Ellemose (2004), p. 358.
21. Stenebo (2009).
22. SvD (26 May 2014).
23. Andersson and Larsson (1988), p. 82 and pp. 325–8.
24. Pettersson (2001), pp. 299–316.
25. Torekull (2011), p. 81 (citation); Interview of Hans Brindfors (2016).
26. Andersson and Larsson (1998), p. 323.
27. Rydenfelt (1995), p. 225.
28. Boje (2004), p. 277.
29. Boje (2004).
30. Ellemose (2004), p. 372.
31. Ellemose (2004), p. 380.
32. Jephson and Morgen (2014), pp. 52–3.
33. Cortzen (1996), p. 32.
34. Cortzen (1996), p. 270.
35. Cortzen (1996), p. 270.
36. Cortzen (1996), p. 56.
37. Lunde (2012), p. 269.
38. Cortzen (1996), p. 280.
39. Cortzen (1996), p. 280.
40. Anförande av Antonia Ax:son Johnson (2009).

6   Blood Is Everything—Succession

There is a saying that every new generation is not primarily inheriting from the previous generation but rather forwarding the fortune to the next generation. This might explain why preparation sometimes can be harsh when it comes to bringing up and incorporating younger family members in the business. There is a wish that the business should stay in the hands of the children or among relatives. Every chance is taken to teach the next generation how to think and behave. Many paterfamilias have been grim when exercising discipline towards the members of the family, especially their own children. The motive is to transfer certain values to ensure that the agenda will continue after the older generation has passed away. Thus, the methods of discipline should be seen in the context of making human investments in the future of the family business.

Mature families face a challenge related to the ever-increasing number of heirs. In case the family adopts the principle of transferring one generation's wealth equally to the next generation and there are a number of offspring in each new generation, it might be a problem, especially when the wealth is not expanding. If some heirs choose to live up their money, only a fraction of the money at the start will remain after some generations. This dilemma highlights some key issues: why stay together as a family firm, who should take the main responsibility for the family enterprise (and most of the controlling shares) and what are the advantages to investing together versus each person taking a share and investing it on his or her own? To illustrate this dilemma; one of the largest family dynasties in India has 23 operating businesses for its heirs, each of whom is a managing director. Only one of the businesses is generating any profit.[1]

The dynasties treated in this chapter are survivors that have chosen keep the control of the businesses within the family. They have overcome obstacles associated with succession of private property and business operations. Some of them have been around for five generations or more. Together they constitute a sterling example of the survival of the fittest. They demonstrate that there are many ways to do succession and that long-term planning is required. This chapter deals with the strategies dynasties have employed to survive without surrendering their controlling interests.

In the normal case, there are heirs in the young generation to choose among. However, a sudden death can upset the best of plans, and sometimes sons-in-law, cousins and other relatives are introduced to take the ball as part of an extended family. Besides, many widows have played a central role in building a bridge to the next generation, as well as outsiders who have been hired temporarily pending maturity of the youngsters. While there are many cases that have caused conflicts and a split of the family interests, there are an equal number with little friction and smooth transfer of ownership and control. The history of the Nordic dynasties provides a rich flora of ways to keep a business in the control of the family.

Family Do or Die

Any succession disputes are resolved by means of an agreement as to who will carry the flame, managing and growing dynastic holdings as time goes on. The Bonniers meet regularly to discuss corporate governance matters, while the Wallenberg dynasty has had a formal family council for many years. It goes without saying that they are anxious to share information, but the imperative to pass down a sense of commitment and work discipline is never far behind. A few select individuals are needed to breathe new life into the dynasty from generation to generation. How are they to be prepared, what schools should they attend, what is the best way for them to obtain experience at home and abroad, what career paths await them?

Biographies of the Bonniers, Johnsons and Wallenbergs make it clear that upbringing and family interactions are crucial to passing down fundamental values. Since the watchwords for the Bonniers were responsibility, quality and the duty to nurture freedom of expression, frequent visits by writers, journalists and other business associates brought children one step closer to shouldering the expectations they faced. The same is true of the Wallenbergs, who also relied heavily on exposure to other parts of the world. Celebrating the birthdays, even of deceased relatives, is an effective way of strengthening relational capital and sustaining commitment.[2]

The choice of higher education and career direction around the age of 20 marks a critical crossroads. Before that point, the younger generation is indoctrinated in the tradition of business ownership and its ideology. That which will one day be expected of them is unlikely to escape their attention. Antonia Ax:son Johnson was told as a young child, "When you grow up, you will take over the business from me. Closed case." Then her father went back to reading his newspaper.[3] She was an only child and anything else was unthinkable.

The Wallenberg saga of the 1970s and 1980s serves as an excellent illustration of the role that kinship plays in determining the locus of power. During Stockholms Enskilda Bank's merger with Skandinaviska Banken in 1971, managing director Marc Wallenberg was torn between the radically different views of his father and his uncle. His preference for the more restrained approach of his uncle, as opposed to the grandiose plans of his father that would prevent uncle Jacob from blocking a merger, only ratcheted up the psychological pressure. He didn't know which way to turn when his father insisted that he serve as vice president of the new bank and eventually succeed Lars-Eric Thunholm as managing director. The day after newspaper headlines announced on 17 November 1971 that Marc had spoken out about a sensitive environmental issue, his father severely reprimanded him at a board meeting. The following day he was nowhere to be seen at either the office or an evening engagement. On the third day he was found lifeless next to his sporting rifle.[4]

He had been plagued all his life by a sense of inadequacy in the shadow of a capable but judgemental father. The frequent recipient of piercing criticism, he struggled on as the bearer of the tradition. The prospect of taking over the big bank that was emerging proved too much for him. Some of his colleagues were not so sure that he was up to the task either. The question on everyone's lips was whether talent mattered or blood was simply thicker than water.

His mother accused her ex-husband of triggering the tragedy by exerting unbearable pressure and many people familiar with the situation chimed in. Marcus's relationship with his daughter-in-law Olga, left to take care of four children, grew frostier than ever. The family had traditionally arranged a major celebration on 19 November, the birthday of founder André Oscar Wallenberg. The date had now acquired a tragic dimension.[5]

Marc's younger brother Peter fled his dictatorial father in South Africa and worked for Atlas Copco, while Jacob's son Peder Sager tried his hand on the board but to no avail. New alliances emerged to make up for the loss of the heir apparent and reinforce the dynasty's influence in the private sector. Marcus Wallenberg made overtures to Pehr G. Gyllenhammar, the managing director of Volvo and a luminary of Swedish industry. By the early 1980s, Volvo's holdings in Atlas Copco and Stora rivalled those of the Wallenberg group. Rumours flew that Marcus was underwhelmed by Peter's potential and had turned to Gyllenhammar as his successor. But corporate governance began to creak here and there and Peter was uncomfortable with his father's juggling act. Claes Dahlbäck, Curt Nicolin and Percy Barnevik contributed more constructively and durably to repairing the rupture with the fourth generation of Wallenbergs.

When the controlling interests were passed down before Marcus's death in 1982, kinship had clearly won the day. His biographer writes,

> Claes Dahlbäck, the managing director of Investor, arrived at Vidbynäs a few evenings before Marcus passed away. The two of them ate dinner with Peter. Dahlbäck noticed that Marcus was overtly friendly to his son for once. He was summoned back out there a few days later. Before they said goodbye, Marcus brushed away any lingering doubts. "If I am not around, listen to my son and nobody else."

And the first thing Peter did was give the boot to Volvo and Gyllenhammar.[6]

Passing on power to a progeny is typically a liberating experience but is nonetheless a complex psychological phenomenon. Godtfred Kirk Kristiansen watched Lego become a global corporation and never had any second thoughts about his son Kjeld Kirk taking the baton from him. In contrast to Marcus Wallenberg, however, Godtfred was anguished at the prospect.

> The most important thing for me has always been to be involved in creating something you can see germinate and grow, and Kjeld would have been better able to do that if he had started on his own. I wanted to spare him. On top of that, it is more difficult to "switch" with your son than with an outsider—in our situation it was not possible to avoid there being both "reason and feelings". If it had been an outsider, I could have made do with "pure" reason.[7]

The alternative would clearly have offered emotional relief. Still, he understood that feelings lend family business their uniqueness by ensuring the kind of commitment that permits ongoing expansion and growth. The biological component is the primary reason that the older generation devotes time and energy to passing down the wherewithal for achieving fortune and success.

However much Godtfred wanted to spare his son, the desire to hold on to the company dictated otherwise. The current potentate can do little more than serve as a role model and instil the principles that will maximize the heir's chances of making the grade. Stern instructions, coldness, cruelty, coaching and kindness are among the many weapons that are hauled out to whip the next generation into shape. Not surprisingly, the targets of such stratagems may feel that they have been unfairly treated, unnecessarily supervised and taken less seriously than they deserve. Ultimately, however, they reap their just rewards when the time for succession arrives.

In contrast to his father and grandfather, Kjeld had formal higher education from Denmark and Switzerland, which might explain the way he tried to develop the firm. He argued that Lego should have strong growth in order to attract employees and stipulated annual growth of at least 15%. His father, chairman of the board, had less sympathy with this aggressive strategy, which was the reason for the long and bitter tension between the two. Godtfred Kirk prioritized concentration of activities and high solvency, and kept an eye on cash flow every day, something his father had always done.[8]

Succession from the second to third generation was a sliding process that took place over many decades. Godtfred was convinced that the firm should neither be listed on the stock exchange nor switch to institutional funds. The firm should entirely be controlled entirely by the family, he declared. After having discussed many ways to transfer control, a traditional form was chosen. Over a course of several years, Kjeld bought his father's shares in the various companies of the Lego group, and became the majority owner of the dynasty.[9]

As in many cases of succession, the grand old man could not stop himself from interfering and nudging his successor. Godtfred Kirk expressed the difficulty of being a pioneer as a delicate matter:

> It is more complicated to make the shift to my own son rather than to someone outside the family. For us it inevitable that there is a true mix of reason and emotions. If we would have shifted to an outsider, I would have been pleased by the rational thought only.[10]

In his new role as vice chairman and controlling owner, Kjeld had a complicated relationship with chairman Mads Øvilsen, who made a statement in the annual report that all communication between Kjeld and the management should take place via the chairman. As the prime owner, Kjeld was frustrated and recruited another chairman in 2008, Niels Jacobsen, to afford himself more influence over the decision-making process. In the fourth generation, none of the three children of Kjeld has any operational duties, besides being committed owners as members of the board of Lego, Lego Foundation and KIRKBI, the family's investment and holding company. "There are clear agreements around the family member's role and responsibilities now and in the future," Kjeld said.[11]

Lonely Spouses and Cracks in the Glass Ceiling

The shipping industry has traditionally been the purview of men with patriarchal lines of succession. Mærsk Mc-Kinney Møller did not go out of his way to shake things up. His wife Emma may have had no career ambitions of her own but vented her frustrations in a letter to the editor published by *Berlingske Tidende* in 1980 under the heading, "The Inheritance from A.P. Møller."

> I have been married to my husband and have followed the shipping company for forty years and have seen how hard he has worked, including in the evenings, when all the green, blue and yellow files have been hauled home. . . . And the long periods away from home, both for businesspeople and seafarers, which was no fun for the family, nor for the children. As far as my husband is concerned, it has been 80 percent for the firm and 20 percent for us. And when they are just gunning for A.P. Møller, and not showing any appreciation, many of us think the men could have spent more time with *us*.[12]

Amalia Wallenberg was equally frustrated when his husband Marcus circled the globe on official assignments during and after World War I at the time their children were starting to leave home. Like many upper-class house-wives, she was bored and dismayed when the elegant business dinners stopped and her offspring flew the coop. A 19 November letter to their oldest son Jacob, who frequently filled in as patriarch of the family, wasted few words.

> I stroll over to the castle, where I sew once a week with 114 other ladies, spend six hours reading for the blind, take a little course at the university. I need to stay busy—it doesn't work to sit there and drown in my own emptiness and misery. At the risk of being accused of exasperation or ingratitude, I am deeply distressed by my lonely fate.[13]

For many years, the Wallenbergs ignored any suggestions that an executive position might suit a woman. Even when daughters claimed their right to assume the mantle of the dynasty, the spirit of the times favoured their brothers. A triumvirate of children were available when Fred. Olsen transitioned from the third to fourth generations. Rudolf Fredrik's daughter Sofie was born in 1913, while Thomas Fredrik's sons were born in 1929 and 1948. Sofie Helene not only could claim seniority but clearly wanted the job. An amendment to her grandfather's articles of association, however, stated in no uncertain terms that ownership and management were restricted to men while women were to receive their slice of the pie elsewhere. The brothers could have quietly revoked the amendment after their father died but presumably could not bring themselves to betray his stated intentions. Sofie felt slighted and continued to seek redress after Rudolf Fredrik's death, but in vain.[14]

She exacted partial revenge at having been dealt a passive role by founding Olsen Daughter AS, her own shipping firm. A court finally resolved the matter in 1970, the year after her uncle died, following 20 years of efforts in collaboration with her husband. Meanwhile her cousin Thomas Fredrik left his younger brother out in the cold on the grounds that he led a Bohemian lifestyle and could not be depended on. The dispossessed young man launched a long and bitter conflict as a bevy of attorneys tried to sort out the rights to the company that the will bestowed. The fratricidal conflict with attorneys running every which way was rich fodder for the gossip columnists. The glass ceiling was finally mothballed in 1985 when Anette Olsen took over the business. Her (sixth generation) children were named Sofie and Thomas in the typical dynastic tradition of using first names to foster the sense of continuity.[15]

Changing Role of Women

The patriarchal nature of Nordic dynasties stems from the kingpin culture of multinational firms that emerged during the Industrial Revolution. As spouses and mothers, women were to take charge of the children and make sure they were schooled to take over the business one day. Not an easy burden to bear. They were also the nurturers and guardians of the social networks that preserved the vibrancy of dynasties. These days women typically become lawyers, engineers and business administrators on the path to top executive positions. Nor is entertainment of business acquaintances in the home nearly as common.

Antonia Ax:son Johnson's ascendancy to the chairmanship of Axel Johnson AB dealt the final blow to the longstanding chauvinistic stranglehold on the dynasty. According to one historian, "The owners managed the first three generations of the company in the spirit of patriarchy, a hotchpotch of centralization, generosity and caprice, as well as tortuous or straightforward decision-making processes depending on the situation."[16] With her liberal arts education, Antonia turned her back on a history of business administrators, economists, engineers and technocrats. She held a number of positions in the group before taking the final step. While notching up a victory for feminism, Antonia consolidated her influence when she married managing director Göran Ennerfelt. If Antonia was an only child, three of her four offspring are women and the fifth generation has even more good choices available to it. Her close relationship with her cousin Viveca also suggests that the dynasty can look forward to a matriarchal future.

Antonia is by no means unique at this point in Swedish history. The third generation of Lundbergs includes the oldest daughter Louise Lindh as the managing director and her sister Katarina Martinson as board member at Fastighets AB L E Lundberg, founded by their grandfather. They are also on the boards of a number of other Lundberg companies. Cristina Stenbeck heads her dynasty but has turned over the chairmanship to an outsider. Nor has she been slow to promote women within the organization. Mia Brunell Livfors was managing director at Kinnevik in 2006–2014, after which she took over at Axel Johnson AB. Eva Bonnier headed up Sweden's largest publishing firm for 17 years until 2007. Annika Falkengren, previous managing director at SEB, broke the ice with the Wallenbergs in two ways, being a woman and coming from outside the family. Most tellingly, men from the family had historically maintained a grip on the industrial banking businesses.

Antonia Ax:son Johnson had predecessors among other Nordic dynasties. Thrine Schibsted jumped in the ring when her husband Amandus died in 1933. For the next 20 years, she modernized the *Aftenposten* newspaper and actively pursued other successful projects until the next generation was ready to assume its responsibilities. She maintained the respect of her colleagues and employees for her ability to hire accomplished journalists and ensure objective reporting.[17] Bitten Clausen, the wife of the founder of Danfoss, achieved a similar status when Mads died in 1966 at the age of 60. He had let it be known that she was his choice for chairman of the board. She never wavered in her confidence that she could do the job and worked closely with management for five years, particularly when it came to the export business. Her passionate fondness for her husband's brainchild was an extra incentive. On her 100th birthday in 2012, she looked back and reflected:

> As chairman of the board, I often travelled with the directors when new contracts were to be negotiated and Danfoss needed to be represented. When we were involved in difficult negotiating situations abroad, for example, and progress was slow in our discussions, the men sometimes held back a little. I was then able to take over the conversation. I had tried that on many occasions when I had to entertain Mads's guests, or when we were on business trips. I actually continued with the role I had had before he died, the only difference being that I now had a formal mandate. Thanks to Mads having involved me directly in company affairs, I was prepared to take on the chairmanship in a way that was close to day-to-day management. In a few cases I also had to go in and sort things out myself, which I was able to do by virtue of my position at Danfoss.[18]

In 1971, Bitten moved over to the chairmanship of the newly formed foundation that managed the majority of the holdings. The initiative not only guaranteed the family's long-term control at Danfoss but was the opening shot for an influential Danish charitable institution. She and her husband had always donated generously to community organizations, particularly during the lean years of the 1930s and 1940s in rural areas. The profits generated by the company permitted ongoing social awareness under the protective wing of the foundation. When her son Jörgen was ready to become managing director in 1996, Bitten could rest on the laurels of a successful childrearing strategy. Peter, her other son, had already chaired the foundation since 1988.[19] She had not only preserved the founder's legacy but passed it on.

Famed for its dictatorial rule at the hands of Ruben Rausing, even Tetra Pak has become more egalitarian as time goes by. Men still control much of the dynasty but their despotic urges appear to have been tamed. The industry has adopted an entirely different worldview, the global market has shifted and a new spirit reigns. Hans and Gad tried to outdo each other when it came to brilliance and the "disciplined imagination" that their father had defined as the most important quality of an entrepreneur. Their inherited stubbornness worked to both their advantage and detriment. Ironically, Hans was most interested in becoming a doctor and Gad an archaeologist. That was definitely an example of undisciplined imagination. "Do as I say or I'll sell the whole shebang," Ruben warned. He saw his image in Hans and made him the prime mover while consoling Gad with the managing director post. He may have turned over day-to-day management, but he remained the working chairman of Tetra Pak and neither son made a move without getting the green light from him.[20]

Joint sibling ownership didn't make it through the second generation. Gad bought out Hans in 1995 and appointed his son Finn as head honcho under the watchful eye of brother Jörn and sister Kristin. One reason for the move is that the grandchildren of the founder didn't get along. Their solution was to provide for as frictionless a succession as possible. Kristin, who is on the board of Tetra Laval along with Jörn and Finn, is among the wealthiest people in the UK.

To conclude, the dynastic role of women has evolved through the decades. For the first few generations, daughters-in-law were more influential than their inborn counterparts, since the latter were mostly serving as hostesses during business representation in the private homes. The ascendancy of equal opportunity has reversed the trend and brought the indigenous family members to the foreground. Research on family businesses has confirmed the depth and extent of the transformation.[21]

Shaky Promises for the Future

Haagen Mathiesen faced two challenges at the end of his life. His company demanded personal responsibility as was typical of the nineteenth century, while none of his children exhibited any interest in shouldering the mantle. He sold all his forest properties except for Hurdal. He still clung to the hope that his son Mogens or another member of the family would eventually want to run the operation. Christopher Thostrup rode in as the knight in shining armour to rescue Mogens and the company. They decided to split the holdings and ran a two-man show at Eidsvold Værk until Haaken C. Mathiesen acquired full ownership in 1893.[22]

Systematic planning and cooperative heirs are no guarantee of smooth succession. An 1893 joint will by Antti Ahlström and his wife laid down the rules of the game. His assets would remain undistributed until his children reached majority and three proxies would run the business in the meantime. It took six years from his death in 1904 for the shares to be evenly allocated among his progeny, with the exception of the small portion that went to his widow. His oldest son Walter became chairman and managing director while the others accepted lesser positions. At the point in the early 1920s that Walter had accumulated better than 40% of the holdings, his siblings put their foot down and resolved not to sell any more shares, just in time to prevent him from acquiring a controlling interest. On two separate occasions, they made deals behind his back to set the dividend yield. Walter, who had been highly successful when it came to both growth and profitability, felt betrayed. After a vote of confidence, he could continue as head of the dynasty. The simple truth was that his sisters understood that nobody else possessed the experience and leadership skills to keep the company vital and competitive.[23]

Gothenburg shipping baron Dan Broström was killed in a 1925 car crash, leaving his wife Ann-Ida and four children. Dan-Axel, his oldest son at the age of 10, was the heir apparent. He had two older sisters but their prospects were less than nil. Until her death 40 years later, Ann-Ida held together the family and all its offshoots, which nourished a generous donor culture in the true Gothenburg spirit. While retaining a controlling interest, she kept up to date about the shipping business but initially turned over management duties to Dan's brothers-in-law. After attending boarding school and studying business administration at home and abroad, her son Dan-Axel joined the board at the age of 22. He was appointed managing director of Swedish East Asiatic Company five years later and ultimately of Ångfartygs AB Tirfing, the parent company. As the result of many profitable years and expanding fleets in the heyday of the Swedish export trade, the group became the biggest employer in Gothenburg. The family, however, brought about its own downfall even before the national shipping crisis struck the final below.[24]

Ann-Ida let Dan-Axel bask in all the glory. He was the anointed saviour who would restore unity to the extended clan. She swept his profligacy and dissipation under the carpet and held the criticism of others at bay with matriarchal resolve. But there was no way she could hush things up when her daughter shot and killed Sten Ekdahl, the first of her four husbands, and served time in prison, nor when Dan-Axel got engaged to his second wife, a nightclub dancer in London by the name of Annabella. Heidi, his third wife whom he met in Acapulco, created less of a scandal.

The offences big and small exacerbated tensions in the family. Erik Wijk, the divorced brother-in-law, went down to ignominious defeat after having called on the Wallenberg brothers to challenge Dan-Axel's hegemony and was booted from the parent company's board in 1960. At that point, Dan-Axel was frequently absent without leave due to the ravages of debauchery. His more level-headed kinfolk had serious plans to replace him but were afraid to do so while Ann-Ida was still alive. The power struggle ratcheted up when she died and he was finally overthrown in 1968.[25] The story illustrates the futility of amity and good intentions when psychological pressure on the crown prince becomes too great to bear. If an extravagant lifestyle is the antidote, the entire foundation of the dynasty may begin to wobble.

Sibling Rivalry

As everybody knows, sibling rivalry often boils to the surface when the time comes to distribute an estate. In the case of dynasties, the ensuring feuds can cripple not only family harmony but the prospects for effective corporate governance. Distinguishing between personal interests and the good of the company can be more difficult. Even if a legal settlement is reached, the emotional scars may be permanent. Subpoenas fly back and forth while legal bills pile up. Succession can be a costly proposition.

One of the more celebrated cases involved the fourth generation of Herlins, the owners of Kone, a Finnish lift manufacturer. On his death-bed in 2003, Pekka secretly willed a controlling interest to his oldest son Antti, who instantly became the wealthiest person in the country. His siblings Ilkka, Niklas and Ilona refused to approve the arrangement while Hanna abstained. The solution was to spin off Cargotec and its 12,000 employees from the group, after which its shares were distributed to the four injured parties.[26]

When Jan Stenbeck died suddenly of a heart attack, the dynastic hold-ings fell in the lap of his 25-year-old daughter Cristina. The existence of an out-of-wedlock child delayed the estate distribution process. Pehr G. Gyllenhammar was recruited as mentor and board chairman of Kinnevik until Cristina had acquired the experience to take over. Simi-larly, the founder of the Axel Johnson dynasty gave up the ghost after a bout of appendicitis in 1910. Either his older son Axel or younger son Helge could have assumed the mantle, but a series of quarrels arose even after they had agreed to joint management. They already had a chequered history when it came to cooperating. Following an abortive deal, Helge accused Axel of having gone behind his back but eventually surrendered his holdings. A letter to his older brother in 1913 illus-trates the fight over the patrimony:

> The main conditions for jointly managing dad's bequest are mutual confidence and fraternal conduct, but—as I knew from the very beginning that, despite all my support for you, I was consigned to a position that did not suit me, either as a brother or as a com-panion, and I was increasingly convinced that it was not so much me but my money and shares that you were after—you will for-give me if my feelings and attitudes have changed a bit. Your lust for power and control of me and everyone else, as well as taking credit for everything, have hardly escaped me, and it was precisely this character trait that compelled you to take the initiative for the failed agreement. [. . .] Your letters were so supercilious, as though I were some kind of farmhand.[27]

Once their collaboration went down the tubes, Axel began hiring outsid-ers instead. He remained the undisputed godfather of the family firm until he died in his eighties in 1958, certain that his sons Axel (the elder) and Bo (the younger) were prepared to follow in his footsteps.[28] But as it turned out, Bo had no choice but to sell his holdings in order to buy Vera, his ex-wife, out of their estate. Vera could have become a partner, but Axel was firmly against turning over any power to "alien interests." Circumstances dictated once again that one son assume the role of paterfamilias. Never-theless, Bo exerted no small influence in the diversified Johnson Group as managing director at Nynäs Petroleum. When Axel acceded to demands that he retire from his executive posts in 1979, Bo stepped in until his niece Antonia could accept primary responsibility.[29]

The disputes that arose when distributing the estate of Hugo and Märtha Stenbeck in the early 1970s and 1980s turned into a public spectacle. The joint will pleaded for the kind of wisdom and team spirit that would preserve and burnish their crown jewel:

> We hope that our children agree that Kinnevik and its subsidiaries are a monument worthy of veneration and protection. [. . .] Let us carry on the business with the dignity and professionalism it deserves. May conflicts of interest be confronted with prudence and common sense and assume their proper proportions with respect for all.[30]

But such exalted ideals came to naught in the wake of endless feuds as Märtha threw her unconditional support to Jan while Elisabeth and Margaretha demanded their slice of the pie. An attempt to stabilize the balance of power boiled down to a limited partnership agreement stipulating mutual right of first refusal for any holdings that were to be sold. The initiative, however, was doomed as early as Jan's passing in 1977, given that Hugo Jr. had predeceased him a year earlier and bequeathed his portion to Jan, leaving him with the same controlling interest as Elisabeth and Margaretha combined. The Battle of Kinnevik lasted for seven years on a field strewn with interminable negotiations and weary attorneys until the Svea Court of Appeal ruled that the standard right of refusal clause was revocable in this particular case. After a few more ups and downs, during the so called Fagersta Affair, Jan wrested control of the shares from his hapless sisters. The family now stood in two opposing camps. Margaretha grew estranged from Märtha while Jan refused to speak with his siblings ever again.[31]

A Two-Man Show, or Maybe Not

The founder or leading representative of a dynasty frequently manages to appoint a successor well ahead of time. Those with widely diversified interests have often required allocating ownership and board positions among various siblings, relatives and in-laws. The goal is always that the centre of power remain with the matriarch or patriarch. Besides pure pragmatism, the arrangement ensures informed decision by scions who can use each other as sounding boards and interlocutors.

André Oscar Wallenberg depended on his older brother Agathon to temper his aggressive approach with caution and foresight. Pleased by the symbiosis, André Oscar urged his son Knut to proceed along the same path.

> It would well behove you to keep in mind the working relationship that Uncle Agathon and I have cultivated for lo these many years.

Everything flows naturally if you start off on the right foot, and camaraderie grows comfortable as an old slipper. And we'll both be looking down on you with smiles on our lips.[32]

He had thrown the gauntlet for the kind of collaboration (historical anchor) that would benefit the business over the long run.

If half-brothers Knut and Marcus Sr. didn't quite live up to their role models, they were able to establish an effective partnership. The wheels began to squeak in the next generation, but Jacob and Marcus Jr. oiled them by assuming responsibility for separate groups of companies. Long-term cohesion was guaranteed by foundations that managed majority holdings through Investor, which turned around and assigned board posts to the various companies. Marc and Peter in the fourth generation did their best but failed to disrupt the continuity, which their children Jacob, Peter and cousin Marcus subsequently reinforced and broadened. The rule of thumb when the time for succession arrives is for the patriarch or matriarch to assign the various positions of influence in the dynasty. The first Wallenberg succession left a couple of the brothers feeling aggrieved while later ones were a good deal less complicated.[33]

With a bank as a platform for restructuring and modernization, the Ehrnrooths were reminiscent of the strategic initiative to which Jacob and Marcus Wallenberg devoted themselves during the same period. Like the Wallenberg aspirants, many Ehrnrooth boys were prepared for future executive roles by means of reserve officer training, higher education and practical experience. The families also collaborated at a professional level that included business deals and the sharing of board posts well into the twenty-first century. Privatbanken, formed with Wallenberg assets and owned and directed by Axel Ehrnrooth in the early 1900s, was the opening shot. A series of Nordic partnership banks were established in Göran Ehrnrooth's time. Based on its passion for renewal in the service of family and country, not to mention the enormous wealth that it acquired by token of long-term thinking, the industrial branch of the Ehrnrooth clan has been dubbed Finland's answer to the Wallenbergs. But the differences are legion.

In the first place, the Ehrnrooths did not strictly adhere to the principle of primogeniture. Their tendency to have large families made it all that more difficult for siblings to buy each other out in order to consolidate holdings. In the second place, the bank formed by the founder proved to be short-lived and the lack of associated industrial holdings aggravated any attempt in that direction. In the third place, they did not have the benefit of Wallenberg's intricate web of foundations, Investor and FAM, a private holding company.[34] None of the four Ehrnrooth foundations for the promotion of culture and science play the same role in corporate governance as those that the Wallenbergs oversee. Moreover, the Ehrnrooths have never developed two-man partnerships even if a host of siblings have reinvigorated the Finnish private sector. In the fourth place, in-laws inherited large industrial and financial estates that substantially padded the family's wealth and holdings. The same cannot be said of the Wallenberg dynasty. In any case, the two families shadow danced with each other across the Gulf of Bothnia.

The existence of multiple holdings to be distributed facilitated the Ehrnrooth succession of the 1960s. Göran the middle son became managing director at Fiskars, while his youngest brother Robert went over to the FÅÅ shipping firm. Casimir, the oldest, grew the Kaukas timber company from an antiquated pulp mill in the tiny community of Villmanstrand near the Russian border to a world-class manufacturer. A carefully planned effort merged Finnish and Finland Swedish industrial assets to form the UPM-Kymmene corporation in the 1990s. A similar deal around the same time produced Merita, Finland's contribution to Nordea, the Nordic banking group. Casimir Ehrnrooth took advantage of his networking skills to help Nokia rise from the ashes by recruiting up-and-coming Jorma Ollila as managing director. Under his chairmanship, restructuring and a new business plan quickly propelled the company to global leadership in mobile telephony and telecommunications, not to mention the biggest enterprise in the country. The current generation of Ehrnrooths own and direct a variety of firms, including Kone and Pöyry engineering consultants, in addition to managing their dynastic inheritance.[35]

The Extended Family

At the turn of the nineteenth century, many privately held firms had been reshuffled into joint-stock companies. Sometimes it was done in relation to succession. When the founder Gustav Adolf Serlachius died in 1901, the family business was in a difficult situation financially, and the future of the main factory—Mänttäfabrikerna—lay in the hands of creditors. At the request of the financiers, the firm was reorganized into a joint-stock company, but succession issues were still not solved. There had been a dispute between the founder and his son Axel Ernst and his wife Alice, which was reflected in the testimony and how to interpret his intentions for the family fortune.[36]

The founder had given his nephew Gösta Serlachius an executive role in the firm. He was prepared for the task by practical training in England, short technical education in Vienna and a study tour in the United States. He fulfilled his duties in a good manner, and in the reorganization of the firm, Serlachius and his wife Sigrid became the largest owners. The two cousins competed for leadership a while until Axel Ernst gave up and sold off his shares. In 1908, succession issues were finally settled and Gösta Serlachius was elected managing director of the firm.[37]

The two next successions went smoother. Erik Serlachius took over after when father died in 1942. He was an engineer and had been the working as his father's closest partner for more than a decade. In 1969, he handed down control to his son Gustaf Serlachius.[38] The story of the Serlachius family reveals a strong element of continuity in terms of ownership and control, as well as planning for long-term survival. The heirs received both theoretical and practical training before they were installed as managing directors. The family unit was used explicitly for investment in human capital to foster professional leadership and an enduring dynasty.

There are also cases with two families that continue to share ownership already from the start. The Kiær and Solberg families can be seen as one entity, since Anders Hansen Kiær married Oline Solberg in the late eighteenth century. Three times, a member of the Kiær family married a person from the Solberg family, which strengthened the ties between them. The oldest son in the bloodline from the first Solberg always shared responsibility with the oldest son from the Kiær family, as a matter of principle.[39] The web of private and professional relationships was characteristic of the bourgeois of the time. It enabled dynasties to carry on international operations while keeping strategic decision-making close to the family.

The family business and its 5,000 employees counted as the biggest Finnish manufacturer when Walter Ahlström died suddenly at the age of 56 in 1931. Despite the absence of succession plans, his brother-in-law Harry Gullichsen was an old hand at the business and gladly accepted the post of managing director the following year. The company fought its way through the Great Depression and World War II, but the effort drained Harry and he succumbed to a heart attack in 1954. Immediate family was available this time to keep the ship afloat and Hans Ahlström presided over rapidly improving profitability and market prospects. Thanks to a number of product and processing innovations, the group assumed its rightful place in the chemical and engineering mechanics industries.[40]

Lars Mikander, his successor, may have been an outsider but he met the criterion of intimacy with the family and its aspirations. He had worked at the company for a quarter of a century. Mikander was succeeded by Krister Ahlström, in the fourth generation from the founder. He experienced that the mill was losing money year after year. In order to keep the pace in the consolidated capital-intensive forest industry, there had to be capital infusions. However, the family did not want to give control to outside investors. The only solution was to sell off, according to Krister Ahlström, but he encountered a compact resistance from his older relatives on the board.[41]

> Not only did I not get their approval, but the members were too upset at the time to listen to the facts [an unprofitable saw mill]. The board was dominated then by the third-generation thinking. [. . .] I was harshly criticized. The mill had such symbolic value in Finland that

many family members were shocked. They thought I was ripping the heart out of the company. Such strong reactions are not unusual in family companies. Their boards often get emotionally involved in management decisions. The care deeply, but they may not always be on top of the business realities.[42]

Krister Ahlström experienced there was a huge gap between the perceptions of the owners and business realities. The problem was not only with the board, since there were 200 families having a stake in the company. "The attitude was 'we have always done it this was. We have always been that business.' "[43] Nevertheless, together with his management team, Krister Ahlström was able to pursue his business plan, pushed ahead and found a buyer, but the decision to sell was only narrowly carried in the board. The sale of the mill was a watershed and started a new life of governance in the history of the Ahlström dynasty. After have been listing the company in 2006, the family retained a considerable interest. Ten years later, it celebrated 165 years of uninterrupted entrepreneurship.[44]

The founder of a dynasty inevitably prays that succession will go smoothly from one generation to the next. Generally speaking, keeping the business within the family grows easier with time as the family tree spreads its branches and acquires in-laws as well. As a result of cousin marriage during the third generation, power in the Andresen dynasty forked out to include the Heyerdahls and Fearnley-Astrups. The controlling interest alternated between the Fearnleys and Andresens while the Heyerdahls were largely content with their commercial law practice. By the early 1900s, representatives of all three branches shared day-to-day management duties. The custom of naming children after their parents and grandparents contributed to the sense of continuity. Either a Nicolai or Johan Henrik led the Andresens for all of six generations, while the Heyerdahls turned to a Jen every other time. Mothers, fathers and siblings, as well as first and second cousins, guarded the extended family's interests in the Norwegian private sector until the Andresens took centre stage in the 1950s.[45]

The Schibsteds also relied on the extended family to maintain cohesion. Holdings were split between two families from the third to fifth generations, after which things suddenly grew a lot more complicated. All according to plan, Christian (the founder) turned the enterprise over to his son Amandus, who signed a joint declaration with his wife Thrine that the family would retain control of the newspaper publishing house. Thrine died and succession culminated with a takeover by the sons-in-law among the Huitfeldts and Lindboes, who proceeded to claim the most important positions in the organization up to the editorial level. Hans Riddervold, an engineer trained in printing as well, stood at the helm of the fifth generation alongside of Tinius Nagell-Erichsen, a journalist with a degree in business administration. Despite the rapid growth of the company, it was still not listed and 16 individuals from four different families divided up its holdings. Hans and Tinius did not see eye to eye when it came to the proper role of the extended family and endless conflicts ensued. It all came down to the importance of bringing in fresh blood to reinforce the legitimacy of the media moguls in Norwegian society.[46]

Hans insisted that the personal owners of a newspaper business had to serve in a prominent public capacity if earning widespread trust was the goal.

> As the largest privately held firm in Norway, we are also responsible for promoting and conducting certain types of associations. Since we are the largest publishing house in Norway, we should care about this institution, an association that our non-socialist readers will cherish. For many, we exemplify the essence of privately based capitalism, and we should not take steps signalling that we do not believe in our competitive edge and authority. We have to hold on to our family tradition.[47]

In his mind, it went without saying that the chairman should be one of the majority shareholders. Tinius argued that it was exactly the other way around. Someone from outside the family was the best guarantee of greater legitimacy. Influential voices spoke out in favour of tighter regulation and control of privately owned businesses. According to Tinius, the drumbeat for regulation would only get louder if the family wanted to keep all the important positions for itself.

> Although the owners might be qualified to contribute to the further development of the newspaper, it is primarily the type of association that guarantees independent editorial boards, not ownership per se. [. . .] If you claim that private property in business life should be implemented such that only owners occupy important positions, I believe that you have hammered the last nail in the capitalist coffin.[48]

His ulterior motive was to silence criticism of consolidation around private holdings. He sought for the chairmanship

> a person who has a firmly anchored vision of or relationship with the lasting cultural assets of society, including newspapers in particular. It should in any case not be a dynamic and tough "powerhouse with success from the fish ball industry," nor a prominent party politician.[49]

A procedural consensus for the chairmanship was two years in coming. The resolution was that the posts at the Schibsted Group and Verdens Gang rotate between the two families. Tinius assumed control for all intents and purposes when Hans died in 1980. The complementary skills of Kjell Aamot, the new managing director, allowed the business to creatively enter the digital era. Tinius did not devote any energy to fostering a new generation but continued to advocate for long-term external ownership while insisting on a large interest for himself. After the Huitfeldts divested their holdings, a listing ensued in 1992. Tinius kept 26%. He inserted a clause in the articles of association that limited individual holdings to 30%. Moreover, three-quarters of the votes were required to amend the articles, as well as separate approval by the kingpin himself.[50]

The Schibsted case is exhibit one of the difficulty inherent to striking a balance among the diverse interest of an extended family, the need for suitable skills and ideological conviction (ensuring a free, independent press). The subsequent power struggle typically leads to a more distinct hierarchical structure that a head honcho from the family sits astride. Tinius sawed off the remaining branches while deprioritizing the cultivation of buds and sprouts for the sixth generation. Just like his forbears Christian and Amandus Schibsted in the early 1900s, everyone called him the newspaper czar. In 1966, 10 years before his death, he surrendered his holdings to the Tinius Trust Foundation. The family no longer had any personal interests, withdrew from day-to-day management and eventually disappeared from the foundation as well. The founding vision of ongoing influence in the Norwegian publishing industry had been shattered.

Sons-in-Law and Trials by Fire

Mærsk Mc-Kinney Møller had three daughters but came up empty-handed on the male side. By the early 1970s, they had all married and he pondered the prospect of grooming one or more sons-in-law to take up the reins one day. Peder Uggla, a Swede married to his youngest daughter Ane, was a naval officer descended from military nobility on his father's side. Unwilling to give up his career, he quickly eschewed any such ambitions. Kirsten had married Mikael Olufsen, the son of chamberlain Morten Olufsen and a friend of Mærsk. Mikael was employed in 1968 and underwent his trial by fire as head of the development division, later as manager of Rosti, a newly acquired plastic processor. Given his forestry training, he was an odd-man-out at the group. After a few years of measly results, he came under heavy internal criticism. "He was willing, but did not have the head and the right training that were needed" was a typical assessment. Mærsk had no doubt had his qualms from the very beginning but didn't want to jump to hasty conclusions. The allure of having a family at the top beckoned to him. Finally he had no choice but to turn elsewhere.[51]

He appeared to strike it lucky with Leif Arnesen, who had married his daughter Leise in 1966. Reports have it that he was articulate, charismatic and sharp as a tack. Educated as an officer, lawyer and business administrator with a Master from Columbia University, he was cut out for the maritime industry. His time across the Atlantic had not only been a close encounter with rules of the game in the market economies, but taught him a language that he could use to woo customers from the head office in Denmark and elsewhere. Mærsk breathed a sigh of relief and bypassed the normal paths to the top of the organization. Leif passed with flying colours and was anointed heir apparent by the Danish press. Mærsk reciprocated by turning up the pressure and dispatching him on long trips to Asia on behalf of the shipper.[52]

Mærsk was demanding but fair with all of his executives. Loyalty and industriousness were the prime virtues he sought. Leif knew how to lead, no doubt about it, but could he really get down to work? By the mid-1980s, Mærsk harboured serious doubts. Leif's acceptance among the inner circle of decision-makers had gone faster than suited some people at the company, and he began to vent his frustration at having to shoulder such a heavy burden. "You don't just have to live with Mærsk Mc-Kinney Møller for 12 hours a day at work, I have to live with him 24 hours a day," he complained to one outside observer. Mærsk was still working near the top of his capacity at the age of 75 and his wife had to content herself with late dinners as always. He religiously showed up at the office by 8 am and returned to work right after dinner while she sat and watched TV. His business travel showed no signs of letting up but she had little desire to go along.[53]

The master was fit as a fiddle but the apprentice was already weary. He wanted to go home at the end of the workday and that wasn't good enough for his slave driver. As Mærsk lectured his employees without a trace of irony, "If they open you up, your blood must be blue, and instead of a heart there must be a seven-pointed star (the logotype of the family firm)."[54] Bjarne Krogh, a right-hand man since the 1970s, took the dictate so seriously that he worked himself to a premature death in 1986 according to his biographer. Leif was the last thing from a workaholic and Mærsk gradually lost faith in him. Once Leif's marriage began to fall apart at the seams and ended in divorce and his 17-year-old son died of cardiac arrest, Mærsk was fully resolved that the dynasty could not be left in his hands. By the early 1970s, both he and Mikael Olufsen were out of the picture. Maerks's grandsons from his daughter in the Uggla family were his last hope.[55]

Culture of Leadership

Many dynasties have intentionally turned to outsiders when seeking senior executives. If holdings are diversified enough, one family is hardly equipped to fill the roster. The Wallenbergs are a prime example. During the lion's share of the twentieth century, they provided a greenhouse for future captains of industry, gradually promoting their finest material within the organization. The entire process centred around identifying individuals with the specific skills required at each step of the way. The managing director of a manufacturer needed to be technologically savvy with a marketing and managerial background. The Wallenbergs and their votaries are known for their networking capacity and exploitation of relational capital.

The correspondence that Jacob and Marcus Wallenberg carried on with their managing directors was integral to upholding and disciplining their team of executives. Thank you notes, an expression of conviviality and *joie du travail*, were also a vital cohesive tool. The tone was often intimate, reminiscent of a father-son relationship. Erik Sundblad, managing director of Stora Kopparberg, wrote to Jacob in 1979, "I looked up to you as the board chairman. You were the best thing that had ever happened to me, you were like a father to me." He deadpanned a couple of years later: "Apparently, our new management team have not had a heart-to-heart communication with you. There was a big mistake."[56] Sundblad was far from alone in his hero worship.

Representatives of the family dispatched their impressions of travel abroad, including concrete suggestions for attractive new markets, customers and suppliers, as well as inviting management to meet with foreign visitors. In exchange, executives passed on information about pricing, the expenditures that competitors were planning and staff turnover. A leak that somebody was about to leave the company could put trade secrets at risk. Executives were never shy about consulting with the Wallenberg brothers concerning requests they received to join various committees and organizations. The answer was almost always a flat no.[57]

The culture of leadership was oriented towards cultivating effective, creative and firm managers. They were also bred to be constructively acquisitive and focused on the best interests of the family. As ambassadors of the dynasty, they participated in the hiring process and used their networking skills to find the most suitable person for the job. Jacob and Wallenberg frequently disagreed over specific matters. They would weigh the merits of the various candidates back and forth until reaching a final decision. Their ability to achieve consensus on fundamental questions was one secret behind the ability of the organization to thrive as well as it did. More often than not, both of them met with a prospective new manager prior to receiving the thumbs up. Any chairman who came from the outside also had to have exhibited longstanding loyalty to both SEB and the family.[58]

Many dynasties constantly use the sense of kinship as a tactic of corporate governance. The owner conveys emotionally charged values that create the impression of an extended family consisting of employees, suppliers and customers. The qualities and feelings typically associated with consanguinity are exploited to ensure organizational unity. Energy and resources are devoted to emphasizing enduring principles and the ideals of the founder as the company expands to embrace global markets and partners.

If Ikea didn't exist, it would have to be invented to illustrate this point. Ingvar Kamprad was quick to say, "We cannot afford to play Russian roulette with the trust of our employees. We must view their jobs as sacrosanct."[59] He solicited strong, determined and humble supervisors who grow with the job and "manage through loves and pats." Friendship, even the experience of being one big happy family, should be their guiding star. He reminisced philosophically,

> As pioneers, we felt a spirit of closeness, both professionally and personally. You could almost say that we were in love with each other. There has never been a happier time. [. . .] I have had the chance to meet thousands of people. I hope I have time for a few thousand more. [. . .] If you like each other, you work to the best of your ability, you hug each other and show your feelings. Not to mention that it's a pretty cost-effective strategy.

He recalled a reporter who asked him about leadership. "When I mentioned love, you could have heard a pin drop in the room, but that's exactly what I meant. You might argue that words are free. My retort is that people don't buy unless they feel good about you."[60]

Kamprad's vision of leadership still ties Ikea's success to maintaining contact with its historical anchor. If the company were to surrender Älmhult, where the first store was set up, and the heritage of frugality, simplicity and hard work to the universe of non-Scandinavian product designers, the focus on distinctly Swedish products would be imperilled. Consumers are attracted not only to specific merchandise but to the unique consciousness behind them. As long as the dream prevails and has its chroniclers, the brand will preserve its competitive edge. The company frequently draws its sustenance from its original roots, and the indefinable spirit of Ikea is suffused with both geography and local culture. New employees from abroad still make the ritual pilgrimage to the milking stool in Elmtaryd, where he grew up: "If Älmhult ever disappears from our heart, both our company and our business concept will sustain a serious, perhaps fatal, blow. Feeling and profit are not mutually exclusive."[61]

Following the death of Ingvar Kamprad in late January 2018, the future of the dynasty was shrouded in uncertainty. The original cult of the individual will live on but the personal leadership that Ingvar embodies cannot be duplicated. As is typical of most founders, he looked to the next generation to selflessly carry on his work: "I don't want my three sons to compete for rank and glory." Meanwhile, he recommends, "Drink a toast and close the deal."[62]

Frictionless Succession

Smooth succession is certainly the standard to which most dynasties adhere. The managing director post at H&M has passed from father to son for three generations without any palpable conflict. Karl-Johan Persson, the grandson of the founder, has been in charge since 2009. The 1974 listing diluted ownership but did nothing to shake the family's grip on one of the most profitable companies in the global industry. The Class A shareholdings and the associated voting majority make sure of that. The choice of Karl-Johan in competition with many older and more experienced employees of the group, demonstrates that kinship is the primary qualification to run a family firm.

The Lundberg dynasty has followed a similar route, ushering two generations to follow in brew master Lars Erik's footsteps without much ado. Appointing his daughter Louise Lindh was an important piece of the puzzle and Frederik Lundberg made no bones of the role played by familial ties: "The tradition of running a family business was always on our lips when we were growing up. The very fibre of our beings absorbed profound knowledge and awareness of what was involved."[63] Louise had similar recollections: "It was always a topic at the dinner table. But I never felt compelled to assume any responsibility for the company. It was an inner voice."[64]

Similarly, Dan Sten Olsson took the baton from his father in 1983 and strengthened the Stena maritime group in the areas of passenger traffic, bulk and carrier transport, real estate, scrap and recycling. Four heirs populate the third generation but nobody knows whether they will become committed owners or simply occupy various board positions.

The Andresens, Due Jensens, Kann Rasmussens, Fazers and Passikivis are additional exemplars of well-oiled succession. Johan H. Andresen is the sixth-generation scion who manages the dynastic holdings throughout the Ferd conglomerate. When founder Poul Due Jensen died in 1977, there was no question that his son Niels Due would succeed him at every key position rather than any of his three daughters. Since the formation of the Poul Due Jensen Foundation in 1975, it has owned 86.7% of the group, along with 2% by employees and 11.3% by the family. Succession to the third generation, at which point Poul inherited the vice president post, went just as smoothly.[65]

In 1992, Villum Kann Rasmussen passed on the chairmanship to his oldest son Lars, who had held various positions at the company since 1964. Succession was preceded by formation of the VELUX public service foundation, which absorbed a large percentage of share capital to ensure ongoing family ownership. Like VELUX, an additional foundation born in 1981, has provided invaluable support to Danish research, development and culture in the areas that the founder envisaged. He died in 1993. When his son Lars Kann began to phase out his involvement in

94   *Blood Is Everything*

2009 at the age of 70, his progeny Jens and Mads stepped in to fill the gap.[66]

Sven Fazer succeeded his father as managing director in the 1930s and handed the business over to his son Peter 50 years later. Succession at Fazer seems to have been without friction. Both the son and grandson of the founder started as trainees, and gradually advanced in the organization, until they finally assumed the role as managing director. They prove to be more than administrators, and the firm grew substantially thanks to mergers and acquisitions. A new factory in 1955, named Fazerila, the purchase of a large Finnish bakery in 1958, a new flour mill in Lahti in 1971 were followed by investments in Sweden, including the Mazetti candy company in 1976. When the third generation took over, the firm was vertically and horizontally integrated, but also more diversified than before.[67]

Dynastic management may be tottering, given that Peter Fazer's successor was an outsider even though he held on to the chairmanship. The family's holdings, however, do not appear to be in peril. Despite the success of the Fazers in avoiding any significant succession-related conflicts, the same cannot be said of its collaboration with Cloetta, another large family business in the chocolate and confectionery industry, early in the twenty-first century. Cloetta Fazer, Swedish-Finnish merger, immediately gained the upper hand in the market, as well as substantial sales in Poland, Russia and the Baltic countries.[68]

The divorce came eight years due to irreconcilable differences over a number of fundamental issues. Fazer's attempt at a hostile takeover in 2005 was a bad omen. The Hjalmar Svenfelt Foundation, which held a controlling interest in Cloetta, responded by citing lack of clarity in the original merger agreement and subpoenaed Karl Fazer Ltd before the Helsinki District Court in 2006. Cloetta argued that the agreement foresaw two large owners that would cooperate in the best interests of the company and its employees, whereas the Fazers had acquired a principal interest and wanted to declare its independence by leaving the stock market. In 2008, management decided to split Cloetta Fazer up.[69]

The case of Passikivi (Oras) illustrates that it is fully possible to implement succession smoothly without violating consensus within the core family. The founder Erkki Passikivi had three sons who all paid attention to the activity of the firm. As young boys, they practiced in the faucet factory and grew familiar with the organization. The oldest son Pekka Passikivi began to work for the firm in 1972 and four years later, at the age of 32, was appointed as vice president, responsible for international operations. His younger brothers later became managing directors within the business. The three sons became shareholders in 1978, after having received a small number of shares from their parents (no daughters in the family). Until the 1990s, the board consisted of four people, the three sons and their father as chairman. The first and the second generation seemed to have shared common views about the direction of the firm.[70]

The firm was already internationalized when Oras started collaboration with Alessi, an Italian design factory, in 2001, in order to develop a well-designed integrated bathroom.[71] The youngest brother Jari was appointed as CEO of Oras Invest and soon became the chairman of the board. At that time, the third generation of the Passikivi family had grown up, and Kaj, Risto and Annika joined the board. Jari Passikivi functioned as a bridge-builder to facilitate succession. Gradually, Jari handed over his duties to Annika Passikivi, who became CEO of Oras Invest in 2011 and the most actively involved family member of the group. Annika Passikivi broke with the tradition of earlier generations in two ways, first being the first woman in the family to reach the top position. Second, she did not agree with her predecessors that an international group could be run from a small and remote place such as the village of Rauma. Therefore, she decided to move the office to the capital of Finland.[72]

Nevertheless, the story of the Passikivis reveals great consensus among the siblings concerning the direction of the family business. They seemed to have shared an understanding of the moves that were made. It was axiomatic from the outset that ownership would be transferred to their sons and daughters. Selling shares was never seriously considered. The decisions-making process was congenial and informal, often as "corridor talks." The third generation called their fathers "the big boys" and were proud to be part of the family adventure. Due to the long-term planning, the third generation was well prepared to take over. The family dealt seriously with the fact that there were more members with ownership interests, for example by participating at international workshops about how to deal with succession, i.e. they prepared themselves for the tasks to come.[73]

Succession at Ecco, the Danish shoe and leather company, was also less problematic. The daughter of the founder Hanni Toosbuy was 20 years old when she became responsible for quality control at a factory in India. From there she started her preparation to take over the role as the head of the company. Accompanied by her husband Dieter Kasprzak, whom she met in India, as CEO, she took over as the chairman of Ecco when her father died in 2004.

Passive Owners Without Day-to-Day Management Duties

Successful mergers of two mature dynasties rarely follow in the wake of strong traditions that have managed to retain the founder's original vision (historical anchor). The history of the unhappy Cloetta-Fazer partnership makes that more than obvious. Nordic dynasties have been more successful at sharing board positions and entering into less formal strategic alliances. Corporate governance frequently focuses on excluding others, particularly families, from the corridors of powers. Among the tactics are refraining from listing, relying on class A shares that entitle the holder to multiple votes or squirreling them away in a foundation. A foundation also avoids conflicts of interest within the family by weathering fluctuations in the wealth or ownership of individual members. Mergers are another story—rarely attempted and even less often successful.

More often than not, mature dynasties send their offspring directly to the boardroom without wending their way through day-to-day management roles. Given the global scope of today's corporations, the managing director position may appear unappealing and stand in the way of other personal ambitions. The split between ownership and management represents a modern refinement of family-oriented entrepreneurship. As long as ownership is active, management will remain subservient no matter how prominence the company's international presence.

The case of Mærsk is the exception that proves the rule. Mærsk Mc-Kinney Møller of the third generation was the prime mover for several decades until his death in 2012. While none of his three daughters were groomed for day-to-day management, the youngest (Ane Mærsk Mc-Kinney Uggla) became chairman of the foundation, which controls the Mærsk group. She obtained a degree in modern languages in Copenhagen, pursued advanced studies at Stockholm University and was a Red Cross Sweden official for 10 years. She served as vice president of the foundation for two years before accepting the top position. Though Mærsk ruled with an iron fist until the day he died, he came to realize that some of his grandchildren were genuinely interested in the maritime industry. After completing university studies, both sons of Ane and Peder Uggla were assigned various positions at various companies. Robert Uggla, who grew up in Sweden, has now reached a level of strategic eminence in the group. The tradition of combining engaged ownership with management responsibilities lives on.[74]

Kinship Triumphs

This chapter has demonstrated the desire of parents to ensure the survival of the business through the contributions of their biological children, or the extended family if that proves impossible. The next generation is inculcated with expectations from a young age and starts preparing in earnest once adolescence sets in. But the pressure is too much for many of them. Plan B is for in-laws, cousins and outsiders to bridge the divide for the duration. The management team can do without an immediate family member for a generation until a great grandchild comes along to pick up the thread. The progressive expansion of the family tree facilitates the recruitment of suitable executives. Because dynastic wealth is increasingly diversified while only a limited number of individuals can serve at the top of the organization, the succession of ownership over time poses a serious problem. Not to mention that sibling rivalry peaks when inheritance is on the table.

The sagas of many dynasties are replete with relationships that are never the same after a parent dies. Identities and roles are shaped and adapted to the demands of the empire and its long-term survival. Women's emancipation from unpaid domestic labour to full participation in the labour market has punctured longstanding patriarchal norms and structures. The trend has accelerated ever since the mid-twentieth century. Fresh blood has reinvigorated the dynasties in the name of equality. Future historians will no doubt look back at the chauvinistic period as a transitional stage that favoured people with training at military academies and universities of technology to serve at large engineering-oriented firms. Current dynasties are reminiscent of the gender breakdown common among artisans at the dawn of the Industrial Revolution before mechanization squeezed women out. Female officers, engineers, lawyers and business administrators with the experience to manage large companies are much more common these days. Patriarchal corporations may turn out to have been as much of a fleeting phenomenon as the industrial era itself. Similarly, the principle of primogeniture has gradually taken a back seat. The relative ages of the heirs to power will, on the other hand, always have a role to play.

Succession tends to proceed most easily when parents have already brought their children or heirs apparent into the business. That way they can gradually let go of the reins and guard their network of contacts less jealously. Fathers who balked at the prospect of losing control are, however, not hard to find. Which doesn't mean that they were reluctant to issue proclamations, commandments and admonitions. Protracted conflicts after the death of the paterfamilias may lead to both tension and aversion where the heirs to the fortune feel as though they are not quite ready to take over. A younger sibling who abjures another career only to find that the business has other plans after all may be overwhelmed by a sense of impotence.

Emotional intelligence is a precondition for the vibrancy of a dynasty. Otherwise the combatants must divide up the spoils or simply exclude one or more of their cohort. Integration of the personal and professional spheres gives rise to a dynamic all its own, a high wire act between emotion and rationality. One false step and the whole edifice may come crashing to the ground. External advisers often ride to the rescue. The new situation may turn out to be either a blessing or curse in terms of the family's prospects for maintaining control of their collective interests. Corporate governance is intimately connected with a ménage that has the maturity to cooperate constructively.

This chapter is replete with examples of well-intentioned wills that be may be legally binding but that fail to rally a discordant bevy of heirs. Occasionally siblings simply carve out their own spheres within the larger conglomerate or agree to sell the entire company as a last resort. Never has a Nordic dynasty voluntarily abdicated or seen a family member that abstained from fighting back against perceived personal affronts. Attempts to outmanoeuvre one of the successors exact a high financial and social price.

The dynasties that survive while maintaining a sense of amity understand that not everyone can poke their heads into day-to-day management and have learned to live with the consequences. The patent solution for ensuring that the family retains control is to place class A shares with superior voting power in a foundation where they are immune from sibling rivalry and unexpected deaths, frequently of burned-out, disillusioned male scions. Vengeful and unsuitable aspirants find it a lot more difficult to engage in selfish activities that damage dynastic power or wealth. The boards of the foundation and group companies are well advised to include outsiders as a means of minimising the risk that family members will base their decisions on personal interests only.

While business strategy is certainly a reflection of both emotion and generational life-cycles, decisions should not be less rational than the deliberations that characterize ordinary companies. Values and the feeling of intimacy are contagious, and vital dynasties are better able to employ these advantages to resolve conflicts within the organization, as well as lay the foundation for both efficiency and creativity. This chapter illustrates the inclusiveness and close relationships that evolve with employees and business associates on the basis of the company's rootedness in a particular family. Ignominious father-son relationships and other deviations can interfere with corporate governance, but strategies informed by unabashed emotional capital may withstand any such setbacks.

Founders and leaders from the old generation sometimes form an autocratic gerontocracy, with no trust only suspicion lent to the younger generation, both family and non-family members. The main reason behind this management style is the dynastic drive that trigger a wish from the leader to stay in power as long as possible. It also seems also to be an element of pleasure of exercising power á la Machiavelli's Prince involved, together with a fear of becoming marginalized once it is relinquished. This gives the historical anchor an extra weight load, in the hand of the head of the dynasty.

Many successors have to wait for decades to reach the driver's seat. At the time of the generational shift, it is likely that a conservative and male-oriented management style has been absorbed by the new generation as part of the traditional corporate culture.[75] Thus, personal capitalism could also be as a sleepy and destructive business, if individual capitalists pay more attention to the company than to the family.

Older generations die out, but the beliefs and principles they espoused live on. A legally binding will may contain ground rules that can be overridden only after long drawn-out disputes, whether in or out of court. The power of a dynastic ruler survives in spirit only. Even the principles he or she propagates may be gone a generation later. But many codes of values are passed down time after time in the light of evidence-based knowledge and the need for signposts to guide corporate governance.

Notes

1. Jaffe and Lane (2004), pp. 85; 89.
2. Lindgren (2007).
3. Anförande av Antonia Ax:son Johnson (2009).
4. Olsson (2000), pp. 374–84.
5. Olsson (2000), pp. 384–5 and Olsson (2004), pp. 90–1.
6. Olsson (2000), pp. 413–4; 435–7 (citation p. 437).
7. Cortzen (1996), p. 280.
8. Lunde (2012), pp. 28–9.
9. Cortzen (1996), p. 267.
10. Cortzen (1996), p. 280.
11. Lunde (2012), pp. 34–8 and Family Business Yearbook (2015), p. 41.
12. Benson et al. (2005), p. 233.
13. Lindgren (2007), p. 92.
14. Hauge (1993), pp. 75–9.
15. Hauge (1993), pp. 77–9; 274–6; 303.
16. De Geer (1998), pp. 454–563.
17. Norland (2011a).
18. Fødselsdagsinterview med Bitten Clausen (2012), p. 2.
19. Boje and Johansen (1995), p. 218; www.danfoss.com/Fragments of Danfoss' History; Fødselsdagsinterview med Bitten Clausen (2012).
20. Andersson and Larsson (1998), pp. 89; 121–2.
21. Karlsson Stider (2000), p. 153.
22. Sejersted (2002), pp. 230–4; 443.
23. Schybergson (1992), pp. 86–8; 119.
24. Mattsson (1984).
25. Mattsson (1984).
26. Hufvudstadsbladet (2009).
27. De Geer (1998), p. 71.
28. De Geer (1998), pp. 68–73 and Nordlund (2006), pp. 245–6.
29. De Geer (1998), pp. 237–40; 428; 444.
30. Björk (2006), p. 235.
31. Andersson (2000), pp. 192–224 and Björk (2006), pp. 234–42.
32. Nilsson (2001), Citation p. 429.
33. Wetterberg (2013), pp. 227–8.
34. A scenario whereby one shareholder has a controlling interest in a company that similarly controls a third entity. As a result, limited capital contributions considerably increase both ownership and influence.
35. Biografiskt lexikon för Finland; SvD Näringsliv (2002).
36. Kontio-Bonsdorff (1969), p. 13.
37. Biografiskt Lexikon för Finland. Gösta Serlachius.
38. Biografiskt Lexikon för Finland. Gösta Serlachius.
39. Sogner (2001), pp. 16–17.
40. Schybergson (1992), pp. 220; 229.
41. Magretta (1998), pp. 118–19.
42. Magretta (1998), p. 119.
43. Magretta (1998), p. 120.
44. Schybergson (1992), pp. 252; 319.
45. Sogner (2012), pp. 148; 293; 510; 516–18.

46. Norland (2011b), pp. 300–6; 381.
47. Norland (2011b), pp. 227–8.
48. Norland (2011b), pp. 228–9.
49. Norland (2011b), p. 229.
50. Norland (2011b), pp. 237; 262; 324; 327.
51. Benson et al. (2005), pp. 205–6; 217 (citation).
52. Benson et al. (2005), pp. 206–7.
53. Benson et al. (2005), pp. 265; 270–1.
54. Benson et al. (2005), p. 267.
55. Benson et al. (2005), pp. 265–7; 271–3.
56. Sjögren (2012), p. 190.
57. Sjögren (2012).
58. Olsson (2000); Sjögren (2012); and Lindgren (2007).
59. Torekull (2011), p. 95.
60. Torekull (2011), pp. 55; 43; 72; 49.
61. Torekull (2011), p. 81.
62. Torekull (2011), pp. 50; 78.
63. SvD Näringsliv (2017).
64. SvD Näringsliv (2017).
65. Ballisager (2007); www.grundfos.com.
66. Boje (2004), pp. 419–23; Berlingske Business (2009).
67. Donner (1991), p. 82; www.fazergroup.com
68. Donner (1991), pp. 79–82; www.fazergroup.com; and Cloetta (2012), p. 29.
69. Sveriges Radio (2005).
70. Herranen (2015), pp. 57–8.
71. Herranen (2015), p. 145.
72. Herranen (2015), pp. 160; 193–5.
73. Herranen (2015), pp. 186; 193–5.
74. Benson et al. (2005), pp. 445–91.
75. Casson (1999), p. 18.

7 Business, Politics and Culture

The living Nordic dynasties are outstanding business groups in terms of entrepreneurship and innovation. However, this comparison of their history also demonstrate that their good relationship with Nordic institutions has been an extraordinarily important factor that has greatly contributed to design regulatory rules of the game that have protected their expansion and success in the region and in the international economy.

Mature dynasties have survived two world wars, waves of nationalization and numerous industrial shocks and financial crises. The external chocks have squeezed private capitalists every now and then and forced them to make a restart. This stresses the role of the government in providing entrepreneurs with effective institutions to build private wealth. Financially, the interwar years were troublesome for most family businesses, but surrounded by stronger business cycles, during two waves of globalization: from the treaties in the 1870s to 1914 respective the internationalization of business from the 1950s and onwards.

In the interwar years, many emerging Nordic dynasties disappeared from the scene and private capital was reduced dramatically. In contrast, the post-war period has been more favourable to private capitalists, but not always. In the 1970s, the attitude towards private profits turned negative even among leading political parties. Some Nordic entrepreneurs choose countries with lower income and corporate taxes, where they registered both their companies and themselves.

History reveals a latent tension between the dynasties and the government. In fact, the history of the Nordic dynasties is also a story of the distance between private money and public interests. This chapter will offer some notions as to the extent to which there has been a constructive state of interdependence or a devastating conflict of interest. Concerning the attitude towards family fortunes, the pendulum has swung back and forth throughout history. Now and then, new institutions have been introduced by a cooperative government to make the world better for private capitalists. However, efforts have also been made to confiscate private capital in favour of government-owned industries. Today, entrepreneurship is highly praised by the government, but this does not prevent representatives of dynasties from fighting for better conditions in order to gain ground domestically and abroad.

In the late nineteenth century, the government actively promoted reforms and introduced legislative and institutional modernization measures, which were important for economic progress, In Finland, Norway and Sweden, the government was active with respect to infrastructure investments and the promotion of industrialization, through building railways, roads and canals. In the interwar period, the role of the government grew, but pathways diverged somewhat between the countries. In Denmark and Sweden, the government's direct control of the economy increased after the 1930s, while intervention was avoided in Finland, although the first government-run companies had emerged after independence from Russia. Self-regulation remained the key principle among businesses. However, the Finish government developed policies to support industrialization as part of nation building, as did Norway after its separation from Sweden in 1905 when the union between the two countries was dissolved. In Norway and Finland, industrialization became a national project, typical for small newly independent countries, where the policies in Norway were directed towards small-scale industries and the policies in Finland, with another economic geography, developed close to the ones in Sweden, towards "big business."[1]

In the early post-war period, the government was active in the birth of the welfare economy and introduced many reforms, especially in the labour market. The element of corporatism and consensus grew in all four countries, sometimes labelled the Swedish model or the Nordic model of welfare economy, with private capital regulated and sandwiched between socialism and the market economy. In the 1980s, the Nordic countries started to deregulate the economy, drifting away from the middle way towards market orientation. Greater tolerance for private wealth followed years of lobbying by private businesses. The change of attitude and policy suggests that the government was convinced of the benefits of having private capitalists. The cause might have been the international shift of the dominant economic regime from Keynesianism to monetarism. However, the highly profitable export sector was an immediate reason for left-wing parties in the Nordic countries to be convinced of the advantages of keeping a strong private sector.[2] Since the 1990s, effective arrangements have been introduced to help private firms open up new markets and the Nordic countries have gained in terms of employment, taxes and budgetary strength.

The chapter will discuss how representatives of various dynasties have made use of the government to improve the climate for their business, i.e., the extent to which the government has been decisive to furthering their fortunes. There will be illustrations of both symbiotic relationships on an individual basis and reactions from members of the dynasties as a response to actions and reforms by the government. There is also a

geographical dimension to all this. We have already noted that many innovative family businesses have started in the countryside. Does this imply
a distance to urban society and the large cities, i.e., to what extent have
private capitalists acted in opposition to a political elite and remained
independent of big finance in the capitals?

Generally speaking, dynasties have used various means to keep ownership control: making pyramids where stakes at the top control enough
shares at the lower levels to hold a majority of the votes, sometimes as
part of a dual-class share arrangement, or setting up family foundations.
In the two first cases, the public can still receive slices of the pie if the firms
are listed on a stock exchange, while the foundation is more of a fortress,
at least if the family-controlled firm is not listed. Historically, the Nordic
countries have approved all three approaches to protecting private capital.

Political Effort and Conservative Resistance

The political interest of Antti Ahlström, a founder of a Finnish dynasty,
was to improve the situation for the Finnish-speaking population in the
countryside, to foster rural development. In the Parliament, he represented
liberals from the village of Björneborg. In two proposals in 1877–1878,
he argued for better schooling for Finnish-speaking children. Another
interest was investment in infrastructure in his region.[3] Likewise, the
founder of Serlachius in Finland was deeply involved in railway policy,
and convinced the parliament to revoke an earlier decision on the route
of a new railway. He also campaigned successfully for starting regular
service for ships on the sea and for the government to invest in national
icebreakers, which promoted the export of forest products from Finland.
In 1896, he was awarded the title of Kommerseråd by Grand Duke Alex-
ander II for his engagement in winter transport at sea.

Dan Broström, during the second generation of the dynasty, belonged
to the liberals and had a seat on the Gothenburg City Council, beside his
role as leader of the shipping firm. He was engaged in the right to vote in
political elections and argued for universal suffrage. He had a seat in the
Parliament until 1911, when he totally became absorbed by the activities
of the family business.[4]

Kiær and Solberg attained a central position in Norwegian society, as
part of both the business and political elites. Peter Collett Solberg was
member of the Parliament for the conservative party from 1897 to 1906,
and Elias Kiær, also a conservative, became a close friend of Prime Minister
Gunnar Knudsen. In the union resolution from Sweden in 1905, Kiær was
active in designing new national institutions and reforming trade policy.
He took part in committees as a representative of the forest industry and
was active in the export association for timber. The business and political
elites were intertwined, and individuals made no distinction between their
professional and private spheres. After a dinner with the prime minister,

who was an engineer, ship-owner and industrialist, Kiær decided to invest in one of Knudsen's ships.[5]

The first two generations of the Andresen family were active in forming the democratic institutions of Norway. The founder Nicolai and two of his sons were all members of the Parliament, and so was John H. in the fourth generation of the dynasty. They belonged to the conservative party. In fact, Johan H. served as the chairman of the party in 1934–1937 and remained on the board until 1945. In the 1920s, he was part of a movement that tried to prevent socialist ideas from being spread within Norwegian society. Later on, he turned more pragmatic and after World War II, he even cooperated with the Labour Party. The fifth and sixth generations of the family returned to a sceptical view of social democracy and established private alternatives to state monopolies (Orkla, private television, and various nongovernmental options as part of Ferd).[6]

The extended Andresen-Fearnley-Astrup family played a key role in introducing institutions that fostered an export-oriented economy in Norway a la Kiær and Solberg. Belonging to the influential bourgeoisie at the end of the century, they set the rules of the game for their private businesses in a relative economically backward country anxious to catch up with its mature industrial counterparts.[7]

Since the time of the founder, the Andresen dynasty has taken a conservative ideological course, for example when private firms were challenged in the early post-war period during a phase of socialization. The representatives of the family argued it was important for welfare society to be market-oriented. This explains why they put so much effort into politics, at least during the first four generations, to match their private interests with democratic principles of an independent Norway. They developed a profound networking capacity, which they used systematically and effectively to obtain support in the Parliament for their private accomplishments.

To Ease the Tax Burdens

The policy of high income and corporate taxes in the Nordic countries has engaged many family representatives. A number of family members have taken a public stand against high taxes. The era of Godtfred Kirk Kristiansen at Lego coincided with the rise of welfare society and a shift towards industry and trade in terms of employment, especially in the rural districts of Denmark.[8] The transformation also meant increases in tax levels and an expanding public sector. After having voted for the Social Democrats, Godtfred Kirk became a critic of the economic policy pursued by the party, particularly Prime Minister Anker Jørgensen. In its export activities, Lego seems to have been hampered by strict currency control; after having waited several weeks for an answer from the central bank, the response was generally negative. Sometimes Lego found ways to circumvent the restriction, even though it was against the law.[9]

Godtfred Kirk was frustrated and claimed that the tax policy did not provide the right incentive for individuals:

> There is one word that has infected the development of Danish society—and that word is taxes. [. . .] Everything beyond a tax rate of 50% is devastating; 50 to the individual and 50 to the government—that is fair. But when the tax rate exceeds 50%, social progress suffers.[10]

Swedish policy currently eases the private tax burdens of large dynasties, including the Perssons, the principal shareholders of H&M, who have received special treatment. Abolition of the inheritance and wealth taxes in the early twentieth century was intended to smooth succession among family businesses. The government was no doubt concerned that their assets would leave the country otherwise. The Parliament has made it clear that dynastic holdings, regardless of their size, are integral to the goal of a sustainable welfare state within the constraints of a democratic market economy.

Mærsk Mc-Kinney Møller, a representative of another Danish dynasty, within shipping, was just as unenthused by high-tax policies. He sympathized with the Conservative People's Party and helped resolve its financial crisis in the 1970s. When the Social Democratic government and Anker Jørgensen turned over power to a coalition headed by Poul Schlyter in 1982, the ship-owner scented the breeze of reform embodied by Ronald Reagan and Margaret Thatcher. His long wish list grew year by year until Schlyter was voted out in 1993 and he lobbied the entire cabinet for regulations and legislation favouring the shipbuilding industry. His correspondence with the prime minister alone included more than 50 letters that ranged from spontaneous whims to detailed recommendations. Nor were they strangers at meetings or dinners, often intimate ones.[11]

Depending on the stridency of the tidings, the tone of a missive could be anything from confidential to formal. Among the typical topics were tax, social security contributions and business policies, valiant attempts to block any aberrations from free market ideology, particularly when they threatened the Danish export industry. When the government joined the boycott against the apartheid regime in South Africa, Mærsk protested immediately. His shipping firm imported coal from the country and the gesture was meaningless from his point of view, only aggravating the Danish balance of payments, particularly because other governments were turning a blind eye when it benefited industry for them to do so. His strict commercial orientation brought down a storm of criticism. The affair culminated with 30 activists from an anti-apartheid group that climbed the fence to his home and held a barbecue accompanied by colourful lanterns, hot dogs and beer but never had the chance to hand him their Racist of the Year award. His wife called the police and the party was over.[12]

Schlyter backed him up to some extent by sending him excerpts from a parliamentary debate about South Africa so he could keep track of what was being said and who was saying it. Nevertheless, the prime minster was frustrated by Mærsk's inability to grasp that a coalition government was beholden to a number of different interests and tried to elicit his appreciation of the business-friendly policies that were boosting the profitability of his company rather than demand the impossible. When they could no longer contain their disagreements, the dispute spilled over to the daily newspapers. Mærsk won the battle when it came to permanent subsidies for the shipbuilding industry, spurring an agreement between the government and Social Democratic opposition in 1986.[13]

Minister of Industry in Denmark, Nils Wilhjelm, who had played a key role in the negotiations, firmed up his credentials with Mærsk when he set up an international shipping register two year later. Vessels flying under the Danish flag could now cut their personnel costs in half by virtue of tax-exempt salaries. After Wilhjelm left the government in 1989 and returned to the private sector, he accepted an offer from Mærsk to join one of his boards.[14] He had shown his stuff when it came to promoting the long-term interests of the dynasty.

Welfare System Alliances

A widespread view is that family businesses do well under Social Democratic governments. The reasoning is that their taxes make it easier to maintain high employment rates, economic growth and the social safety net, narrowing income deficiencies and pacifying the population. The incentive to privatize is less if business profits continually replenishes government tills.[15] The thesis may be shaky with regard to the postwar period until the 1970s when welfare systems expanded rapidly and businesses had to either relocate or otherwise evade high taxes, whether legally or not. The ability of the government to ensure sufficient public consumption was seriously compromised. As of the 1970s, however, the theory works quite well. The empirical evidence is hard to dismiss—many large family businesses, particularly in Norway and Sweden, have seen the light of day when the Social Democrats were at the helm. The government and barons of industry have decided to sit in the same boat and synchronize their rowing strategies.

The Swedish model and welfare state after World War II were based on a manufacturing sector that was operating at full capacity and could absorb throngs of new workers from home and abroad. Increases in corporate, wealth and inheritance taxes as part of a reform engineered by Swedish Minister of Finance Ernst Wigforss in 1947–1948, however, dimmed prospects for profits and the accumulation of personal fortunes. Given that one objective of the planned economy espoused by the labour movement was redistribution of wealth to the public sector, the motivation was not only fiscal in nature. Such radical socialism was a direct threat to dynastic life expectancies. The Johnson Group lost no time in transferring some of its holdings to safe harbours at hastily constructed foundations.[16]

The idea of nationalizing the public sector gradually faded and Swedish Minister of Finance Gunnar Sträng led a realignment of fiscal policy to satisfy the wishes of big companies in hopes of keeping jobs from fleeing Sweden. The Social Democratic government preferred cobbling together guidelines with a handful of private sector representatives to negotiating with a host of entrepreneurs and small businesses. The big caps continued to dominate manufacturing accordingly, while start-ups short on assets found themselves in a much more difficult position. The long- and short-term bond markets were the primary source of capital as the Stockholm Stock Exchange languished and even faced calls for closure from some quarters. The symbiosis between the government and big money nourished the welfare state. Typical of the times, Sträng and Marcus Wallenberg sat down and charted a vision for the future of Swedish industry. Marcus and Prime Minister Tage Erlander were regarded as head honchos of the private and public sectors respectively. But also non-Wallenberg companies rode the wave and obtained more lenient fiscal regulations in exchange for investing in Sweden and protecting jobs.[17]

Research has shown that fiscal policy encouraged debt financing as opposed to new share issues until the early 1990s, an advantage for Handelsbanken and Wallenberg enterprises and their in-house banks.[18] Given that expansive new businesses and aggressive entrepreneurs encountered major headwinds, founders of dynasties such as Ingvar Kamprad (Ikea) and Ruben Rausing (Tetra Pak) registered their companies in countries with more inviting fiscal conditions. In the 1990s, the European Commission questioned the Swedish practice of weighting voting power by means of class A and B shares (dual voting shares). Jacob Wallenberg and Prime Minister Göran Persson put their heads together and convinced the authorities to leave things the way they were. The alliance between the government and industry was as strong as ever.

A Long Tradition of Mutual Benefit

Back in the old days, André Oscar Wallenberg, the founder of the Wallenberg dynasty, employed an entire arsenal to ensure a platform for the banking system he envisaged and jump start his own institution. He joined with Minister of Finance Johan August Gripenstedt to score a number of successes for his dream of a new free enterprise system, paving the way for loans to rapidly advancing innovative firms. They exploited both law and public policy in the service of the economy to string together various types of national and international collaborative projects. Their networking skills facilitated the adjustment of legislation to serve the needs of burgeoning industrial society and uniformity within larger geographic areas. The institutions they engendered promoted long-term confidence by launching and legitimizing negotiable short-term investment credits and other financial stimuli.[19]

Finnish founder Carl Albert Ehrnrooth also manipulated the political system to change the rules of the game in his industries. His appointments as undersecretary at the Ministry of Agriculture in 1862 and Ministry of Finance provided perches from which to advances interests that helped his own businesses as well. He was also chairman of the Finnish Agricultural Society, as well as a board member of insurance and mortgage companies involved in such issues. As vice governor of the central bank, he could monitor the economy at close range and plan measures that would accrue to his own advantage.[20] By virtue of his noble heritage and networking savvy, he made the personal the political and vice versa in an era when a small coterie of individuals drove the Finnish private sector and parallel careers were a realistic option.

With his equally oversized personality, Jan Stenbeck lobbied Swedish politicians fast and furiously in the late twentieth century. His companies have also taken advantage of the revolving door and hired former officeholders to keep an eye on public policy developments. Accepting public appointments the way the Ehrnrooth and Wallenberg patriarchs had done would have been neither plausible nor efficient. Both Odd Engström and Björn Rosengren, former vice Prime Minister and Minister of Enterprise respectively, have served as consultants and belonged to inner dynastic circles. More recently, Minister of Finance Pär Nuder has been working for the Wallenbergs. Former Minister of Finance Anders Borg became vice chairman of Kinnevik, the crown jewel of the Stenbeck dynasty. These people know the ins and outs of the political system, as well as how to get in touch with officials and venues around the world.

When Bonnier set out to purchase TV4, the only privately owned public service channel in Sweden, conversations with the Ministry of Culture were key to its success. The year was 2007 and the Centre-Right Alliance government was early in its four-year term. In accordance with the Swedish Radio and Television Act, Bonnier's ownership structure and interests could not change such that it would exercise significantly greater influence on the mass media.[21] The purpose of the provision was to ensure diversity in shaping public opinion and enable public service channels to monitor the powers-that-be on the basis of competing social and political standpoints. Contravention of the conditions would result in revocation of a channel's broadcasting licence. The Government was responsible for reporting suspicion of any such violation and launching an inquiry. In other words, additional concentration of influence could easily be blocked without passing new legislation. Minister of Culture Lena Adelsohn Liljeroth, however, filed no such report and Bonnier was able to purchase TV once the Swedish Competition Authority had given its stamp of approval. Meanwhile, the Parliament adopted a law entitling the channel to air 50% more advertising, a boon to Bonnier's bottom line. Spearheaded by former Minister of Culture Marita Ulvskog, the Social Democratic opposition was highly critical, but the government chose obeisance to the powerful publishing house.[22]

Dynasties have clearly helped construct the capitalist system to which the West subscribes. Their reform efforts have challenged monopolies and explored virgin territory. Virtually on their own, they have spawned new markets. The Bonniers, Ehrnrooths, Kristiansens, Mærsks, Perssons, Stenbecks and Wallenbergs, among others, have revitalized the private sector and communicated with politicians to advance their own agendas. Instead of taking institutions for granted, they have rolled up their sleeves and actively promoted new rules of the game. Every market is subject to its own tenets and traditions, and the dynasties have realized that change is vital to their own prosperity and survival. That way they have set the stage to keep their crown jewels polished and appealing. The have secured the mode of the historical anchor without lifting it up.

Give and Take—a Question of Culture

There is little doubt that dynasties have exploited their alliances with external companies and executives to retain and strengthen controlling interests. But such partnerships and loyalties have also extended to elected officials. Conglomerates that guarantee high employment rates for Swedes have learned to see eye to eye with various political parties and entered into a contract with the general community. Taxes, employment and philanthropy are the price families have paid for regulations that favour inheritance and government protection of large private fortunes.

A social contract has legitimized dynasties and gradually propelled the dynasties into ever greater prominence and esteem. This contract also includes philanthropy, as a tool for dynasties to stay connected with their surroundings and strike the pose of benign capitalists in the eyes of officials and the general public. As a matter of fact, the Nordic dynasties have come to be major donors and philanthropists.

With annual contributions equal to the entire Swedish GDP, the United States is the leading example of charity as a vital arm of capitalist economies. Sweden boasted of a similar culture in the early twentieth century but saw many private fortunes wiped out during the deflationary crisis of the 1920s and the subsequent Great Depression. Whatever remained was extinguished in the wake of wealth redistribution, high income and corporate taxes and regulation of capital markets following World War II. Deregulation, along with abolition of the inheritance and wealth taxes, of recent years has resuscitated the spirit of giving. Many dynasties make substantial contributions to research, education, infrastructure, health care, religious institutions and welfare organizations.

The third and fourth generations may have an entirely different view of the world once they have amassed considerably wealth. As an example, fourth generation scion Viveca Ax:son Johnson of the Johnson dynasty commented during an interview with the *Dagens Industri* financial daily, "The founders were almost obsessed with the concept of entrepreneurship. I want us to us to play more of a public service role. You can't hoard everything forever."[23] The Axel and Margret Ax:son Johnson Foundation for Philanthropic Purposes gives her as chairman and her mate Kurt Almquist as managing director the opportunity to make her dream come true.

Families frequently constitute a vortex of power from which to manage investments and exercise influence by virtue of board posts with associated companies and organizations. The transfer of wealth to foundations is a smart strategy in more than one way. By funding educational, research and cultural institutions, they increase their legitimacy and raise their status. The display of social responsibility also strengthens the brand. Besides, by its very nature, a foundation contributes to the survival of a dynasty by minimizing dependence on family members who currently sit at the top of the totem pole. A greater sense of cohesion stems naturally from its inviolability.[24]

Notes

1. Fellman and Sjögren (2008), pp. 566–7.
2. Sjögren (2012).
3. Schybergson (1992), pp. 53–5.
4. Mattsson (1984), pp. 43–5.
5. Sogner (2012), pp. 58–9.
6. Sogner (2012), pp. 335–54; 517–23.
7. Sogner (2012), pp. 166–203.
8. Iversen and Andersen (2008), p. 309.
9. Cortzen (1996), pp. 267–8.
10. Cortzen (1996), p. 267.
11. Benson et al. (2005), pp. 274–7.
12. Benson et al. (2005), pp. 276–82.
13. Benson et al. (2005), pp. 283–8.
14. Benson et al. (2005), pp. 290–1.
15. Sogner (2012), pp. 522–4.
16. De Geer (1998), pp. 209–20.
17. Olsson (2000), pp. 339–40.
18. Henrekson (1996), pp. 63–4.
19. Nilsson (2005).
20. Komulainen and Siltala (2016), p. 6.
21. SOU (2004), p. 104.
22. Dagens Nyheter (2007); Journalisten (2007); and Aftonbladet (2010).
23. Dagens Industri (2015).
24. Wetterberg (2013), pp. 227–8.

8   Conclusion

The Nordic countries would have been much less affluent without the dynasties they spawned. These families brought market economies to the region during the Industrial Revolution, leading the way to export breakthroughs and growing prosperity. The dynasties rebuilt the countries when the rural areas were dynamos of growth and they drew their sustenance from entrepreneurship outside the urban centres. The new and vibrant dynasties that emerged in the wake of the world wars helped the old ones create jobs and wealth in many expanding industries. Even the younger dynasties have enriched the Nordic countries, and the way that family businesses pursue their activities has a direct impact on society's economic fortunes. Why have so many large, successful family businesses emerged in the Nordic countries? And what is the reason that firms whose owners remained anonymous (or firms with diluted ownership) have been unable to survive or grow as rapidly over the long run?

The short answer to the first question is that public policy has permitted private fortunes to accumulate within the country ever since the heyday of free enterprise during the Industrial Revolution. Neither government regulations nor attempts by the labour movement to restrict private ownership have fundamentally altered that calculation. Therefore, they also bring economic inequality to the world, unfortunately.

The short answer to the second question is that market economies rooted in family businesses appeal to both reason and emotion in a way that ultimately benefits the majority of entrepreneurs. Kinship evokes an extraordinary level of commitment. As rationally as these businesses may be run, the decision-making process is also informed by feeling. Far from being commercial enterprises, they are a venue for power, philanthropy, passion, conflict, freedom and captivity. The key to endurance is the ability to adapt to the changing internal and external environment. That adaptability is a necessity for their longevity.

As long as it is properly nurtured, their brand of capitalism is the heart that pumps blood into the veins of the greater community. However, personal, demonstrative impulses must be reined in such that the competitive instinct is reignited in each generation and everyone involved can make a clear-eyed determination as to the individuals who possess the where-withal to take over once the time has come to pass on the baton. Striking a proper balance generates a credible narrative that people can create an incubator of wealth that will survive into the distant future and provide stimulating challenges to new generations. The narrative is a source of not only fascination, encouragement and paradigms, but also self-esteem and intangible rewards for having performed the arduous tasks that such businesses demand.

The values that the Nordic dynasties articulate and uphold have been linked to the Protestant Ethic—work is a calling, income is to be saved and reinvested, and moderation is to reign supreme in every other sphere of life. The initial triumphs of dynasties are based on temporary monopolies born of an invention. A single ground-breaking innovation in a particular sector is typically enough to nurture the growth of a far-flung empire. Such discoveries are subsequently upgraded, refined with new technologies and disseminated to many different industries. Survival in the market also requires ongoing entrepreneurship characterized by constant renewal on the part of employees as well (intrapreneurship). A ground-breaking innovation marks a departure from accepted institutions and industry practice in a more visionary way then businesses without conspicuous owners can hope for. The founders persuasively communicate their aspirations—employees are told why the business proceeds in a particular manner while customers learn that the products and services are associated with an overarching concept and specific corporate culture. Personal leadership opens the door to many sources of identification that serve as a gravitational force in the market.

By laying down a historical anchor and engaging in private risk-taking, family businesses cultivate a greenhouse in which ownership can strike root and grow. The need to reshape market conditions dictates that they become lobbyists or establish close ties with elected officials and public policymakers. The dynasties forge new markets, rewarding the economy with an ever-widening pool of jobs. Their status as major employers and bulwark of the labour market has cast them into the maelstrom of politics. As long as they play the part of obedient capitalists who contribute to national prosperity, special tax benefits and other regulatory advantages come their way. Owners join the establishment and amass political capital with both policymakers and the general public as they strive to promote their brand on the behalf of both themselves and their business.

In the long perspective, business owners won the support of the political system by virtue of the employment and export opportunities they provided. Even the Social Democrats, who long dominated the Nordic governments, acknowledged the contributions the pioneers made to the region's material prosperity. The welfare state and Nordic model entwined capital and the public sector in close symbiosis at an early stage. The labour movement and private sector understood that the country would profit from a common roadmap. Slowly but surely, the Nordic dynasties demonstrated their dynamic, incomparable capacity to promote widespread affluence.

Nordic institutions have greatly contributed to the survival of large family firms, since the nation states have provided favourable rules aiming to protect their expansion over time. However, such incentive structure and centralization of power encourages monopolistic economies and inertia that frustrates entrepreneurship. Alliances between leaders of industry and government representatives may be detrimental to consumers in small countries as Denmark, Finland, Norway and Sweden. The determination of the family to maintain its control of a company at all costs can lead to a brain drain as less competent members of the clan squeeze their way past outsiders. Nepotism is always lurking around the corner. Hopefully the ascendancy of women to executive positions is a sign of more liberal and inclusive management. The pool of candidates for top positions has doubled as a result, while the future promises even more reliance on skills acquired from higher education and oriented towards performance.

The Weight of Tradition

The tendency towards paying exaggerated reverence to tradition is also on the negative side of the dynastic ledger. The conservatism that finds expression in unquestioning acceptance of previous strategies can hamstring new ideas and impulses, ultimately lending an advantage to ordinary companies. History is chock-full of dynasties that have lost their economic and significant consequence, lapsing into a state of virtual hibernation.[1]

Particular when it comes to shipping, shipbuilding and textiles, holdings have been restricted to industries that became less competitive with the rise of globalization. Other times the family has lacked the skill and financial muscle to retain a controlling interest. Two critical factors have been liquidity and the ability to hire qualified, motivated people with the spirit of entrepreneurship. In their absence, boards have become crusty and fearful of making the kinds of long-term investment decisions demanded by the weaker market. They have simply lacked the ability to adapt to the changing internal and external environment.

Ultimately, however, it all goes back to the weight of tradition (historical anchor), which both affords stability and narrows the scope of action. Stability consolidates structures that may obscure opportunities for satisfying fresh needs as they arise. A generally accepted truism is that corporate culture must change before new strategies can be truly effective. In other words, a dynasty must be prepared to let go of tradition every once in a while and drift with the tides of the time. If not, the next recession can easily drag the company down into the murky depths of the past.

Navigating the shoals of change correctly requires the proper balance of emotional detachment and professional commitment to tradition. Obtaining assistance of business experts and scholars of industrial dynamics can shake off some of the barnacles, leading to a higher degree of flexibility and organizational dynamic. Family councils can do a lot but various institutions specialized in planning and carrying out succession even more. Independent advisors help channel feelings more constructively and ease the way.

The Future of Dynasties—Local Is Global

Where will future dynasties be born and what industries will they tackle? Many have arisen in small towns and rural communities. Considering that it is still cheaper to build plants and office buildings there, it is certainly not a thing of the past. Ingvar Kamprad said, "When I speak of the Ikea family, I always have country life in mind. That's where I drew inspiration for my ideas of togetherness and mutual interdependence, that's where we lived our own truth in a protected microcosm."[2] In the digital economy, the countryside has the potential to serve as a rich source of the values that inhabit every vibrant dynasty.

Even in the age of information, where everyone is online regardless of geographical location, land and physical premises are needed to run a business and distribute the goods and services that have been ordered online. Besides, in the rural area it is closer to raw material, including the sea. For many firms, the need for highly skilled workforce in the metropolitan areas, with university education, is not always intrusive, as companies are engaged in scaling up handicrafts and low-tech.

Payroll and living expenses are generally lower outside the metropolitan areas, not to mention that employees are more loyal when that know that ownership is in local hands. Municipalities that long for businesses to create job opportunities in a region are eager to improve and expand infrastructure, airports, housing and other amenities to accommodate them. The real challenge emerges when the company grows to the point that it operates abroad as well. Can business models and values be translated to other cultures and consumer traditions, provide a competitive edge and anticipate the curve of the market?

A common wish among family business people is freedom and self-determination, to be able "to run the case in their own hands." A family business that relies on shareholders' equity for development is only minimally dependent on metropolitan financial centres. On reason that Warren Buffet decided to locate in Omaha was to ensure autonomy from Wall Street and the establishment. During various periods, the Gnosjö Region, on the countryside of Sweden, has accounted for the greatest number of business starts and new employees in Sweden by virtue of its entrepreneurial culture.[3] Having many family businesses in the same area knits up the region in a network of shared values. Proximity to national financial centres is far from a requirement for budding dynasties and may actually be a hindrance if independent ideas and unique relational capital are on the agenda.

What also makes the future of family dynasties bright is the change of the financial system. When banks were the major or only source of external finance, especially in Europe, the family firms could easily lose their independence and succumb to the entrenched power by the mighty industrial banks. Since the 1980s, the capital market has been open, sophisticated and large, which gives the family firms better access to the financial market without losing experiencing a loss of family control.[4] Second, to be local is not a contradiction to stay global. Many family firms use their network capacity for wide-ranging internationalization, where they can focus on one or more niche products. The coherence of a family firm is a way a managing risk in a high-risk environment, where the political and institutional risks are less than before. In the first twenty-first century's globally transformed markets, the risk is limited to holding the pace of the digitalization of the economy, i.e. a risk of not updated technologically.

Third, a tranquil, organized approach is normally a winning concept, as opposed to setting quarterly targets and constantly peeking at the bottom line to see whether they being met. Farsightedness usually pays off for both the company and the overall economy. A 2017 study of listed American companies found that those with a broader horizon outgrew others by 36% in terms of profits and 47% in terms of earnings from 2001 to 2014. They also averaged 50% more expenditures on research and development as well as contributing many more jobs. They ploughed ahead with their R&D efforts during the financial crisis and recession of 2007–2009. Largely as a result, their market cap rose relatively quickly once the economy was back on its feet. If all businesses had followed in their footsteps, 5 million more jobs would have been created and GDP would have been a trillion dollars higher.[5]

Family businesses that offer competitive niche products on the global market, so called pocket multinationals, have a solid platform from which to grow. They continue to have the capacity to draw entrepreneurial profits. That conclusion is applicable not only on the periphery of Europe with their welcoming entrepreneurial climate, but also in many emerging economies. As long as society is organized around families, such businesses will have a natural role to play. While mature dynasties have a distinct lead, particularly now that the inheritance and wealth taxes have been abolished, a family can establish a powerful international presence in the matter of one generation.

In the age of globalization, access to skills is unlimited. As companies expand and formal expertise grows in importance, interests outside the family may seem to have stronger ownership claims. But that's not the way it works—while businesses come and go, dynasties are a permanent fixture. Institutions as they are now structured in most of the world favour entrepreneurship and the accumulation of private capital, as well as the transfer of assets from one generation to the next. As an example, family firms can generate better access to market capital because they create a relational capital of trust that offers a response to market failure.[6] Moreover, kinship is a greater qualification in professionally managed family businesses than education or experience.

The Asian economies neither copy the Anglo-American traditional corporation, nor wait for state-led initiatives, as many European firms have done. They rather tend to draw on the dynamic and entrepreneurial family firm for value creation and economic growth. However, the process towards family capitalism needs liberal rules of the game. Consequently, the strong growth of family groups in India came because of deregulations starting in the early 1990s. By liberalization of state-controlled economies, as China, we could expect the emergence of many more family firms, of which some will soon become dynasties.

Notes

1. Among Swedish examples are the Broströms (shipping), Kempes/Carlgrens (forestry), Kockums (shipbuilding), Marks and Carlanders (textiles and ball-bearing), Wehtjes (construction and cement), Åhléns (department stores) and Saléns (shipping).
2. Torekull (2011), p. 71.
3. Ds (1992), pp. 80–1.
4. James (2013), pp. 77–9.
5. McKinsey Global Institute (January 2017). Long-term businesses emerge on the back of five different variables: investment, earnings quality, margin growth, quarterly management and earnings-per-share growth (Corporate Horizon Index Methodology).
6. See also James (2013), pp. 80–1.

Epilogue

Why bother writing a scholarly history of dynasties when it would have been just as easy to come up with suspenseful fictional account? It would have saved the hard work of assembling source material, reviewing the literature, checking the facts and putting together footnotes. One reason for sticking to historical objectivity is that the family has requested that the chronicle to be written. However, academic research should be even more ambitious than that.

The best argument for a factual rather than a fictional approach is that it permits a greater understanding of our trajectory to the present state of the world. An academic analysis reveals the patterns of cause and effect as they play out in each generation, the power of human agency to forge both temporary and permanent values and principles. The lines between that which is possible and that which exists only in the realm of the imagination become clearer. Systematic cases studies proceed from empirical data to draw general conclusions and devise theories from ostensibly isolated occurrences.

The potential for accomplishment within one or several generations suddenly lies open to view. The dynamics that propelled the Nordic countries to the top of the global economic hierarchy begins to crystallize. Each generation, whether members of a dynasty or not, must gather this information and learn these lessons anew in order to meet the challenges of today and tomorrow.

I would like to express my gratitude to Annette Forsén, Martin Jes Iversen, Markku Kuisma, Mattias Nordqvist, Knut Sogner and Rikard Westerberg for reading my drafts so carefully and for their valuable comments.

Thank you, Paloma Fernández Pérez and Andrea Colli, for our conversations in Barcelona and Milan, and for many constructive comments on earlier versions.

Thanks to Håkan Lindgren for having unerringly followed my research and served as a loving mentor since 1987 and for having taken the time once again to peruse my manuscript.

Thank you, Anders Perlinge, for your grammatical corrections and for detecting misspellings and typos that all the word processing programs miss.

Thanks to Tino Sanandaji for launching and conducting a statistical study of the largest international family businesses, as well as for your constructive criticism of my manuscript.

I would like to extend a special note of gratitude to the Heckscher Institute (EHFF) at the Stockholm School of Economics. The institute remains an invaluable and ever deeper source of knowledge and creativity for all economic historians.

Thank you, Ken Schubert, for translation and your scrutiny of the language.

Thank you, Heather Forsyth, my love, for your patience with all my travel abroad, and for your many good ideas.

The Swedish Foundation for Humanities and Social Sciences financed research and translation. Grants from the Handelsbanken Research Foundations and the Royal Patriotic Society permitted this book to be printed.

Linköping and Milan
February, 2018
Hans Sjögren

References

Aftonbladet (12 November 2010), "Borgarna + Bonnier = sant", signerad Johannes Wahlström och Dan Josefsson.

Andersson, Per (2000), *Stenbeck: Ett reportage om det virtuella bruket*. Stockholm: Norstedts.

Andersson, Peter and Tommy Larsson (1998), *Tetra: Historien om dynastin Rausing*. Stockholm: Norstedts.

Anförande av Antonia Ax:son Johnson i Seglora Smedja, digital version published 2 December 2009.

Arregle, Jean-Luc, Michael Hitt, David Sirmon and Philippe Very (2007), "The Development of Organizational Social Capital: Attributes of Family Firms." *Journal of Management Studies*, 44(1): 73–95.

Ballisager, Olav (2007), *Grundfos—mere end pumper*. Grundfos Management.

Benson, Peter, Bjørn Lambek and Stig Ørskov (2005), *Mærsk. Manden og magten*. Köpenhamn: Politiken Bøger.

Berlingske Business, "Sønner till tops i VKR-koncernen", 17 May 2009. Köpenhamn.

Biografiskt lexikon för Finland. Helsinki.

Björk, Stellan (1998), *Ikea. Entreprenören, affärsidén, kulturen*. Stockholm: Svenska förlaget.

Björk, Stellan (2006), *Dynastin Stenbeck. Succéer och tragedier i en finansfamilj*. Stockholm: Svenska förlaget.

Boje, Per (2004), *Villum Kann Rasmussen. Opfinder og entreprenör*. Köpenhamn: Gyldendahl.

Boje, Per and Hans Christian Johansen (1995), *En iværksætter. Historien om Mads Clausen og Danfoss*.Odense: Odense Universitetsforlag.

Brundin, Ethel, Emilia Florin Samuelsson and Leif Melin (2008), "The Family Ownership Logic: Core Characteristics of Family Businesses." *Jönköping International Business School*, Centre for Family Enterprise and Ownership, Working Paper: 1.

Carlsson, Rolf (2001), *Ownership and Value Creation: Strategic Corporate Governance in the New Economy*. Chichester: John Wiley & Sons.

Carlsson, Rolf (2007), "Swedish Corporate Governance and Value Creation: Owners Still in the Driver's Seat" *Corporate Governance*, 15(6): 1038–55.

Casillas, Jose, Francisco Acedo and Ana Moreno (2007), *International Entrepreneurship in Family Business*. London: Edward Elgar Publishing.

Casson, Mark (1999), "The Economics of the Family Firm." *Scandinavian Economic History Review*, 47(1): 10–23.

120   References

Cloetta (2012), *Cloetta 150 år 1862–2012*.

Colli, Andrea (2003), *The History of Family Business*. Cambridge: Cambridge University Press.

Colli, Andrea (2016), "Personal Capitalism", in: John Wilson, Steven Toms and Abe De Jong (eds.), *The Routledge Companion to Business History*. London: Routledge.

Colli, Andrea and Fernández Pérez (eds.) (2013), *The Endurance of Family Businesses: A Global Overview*. Cambridge: Cambridge University Press.

Corbetta, Guido and Carlo Salvato (2012), *Strategies for Longevity in Family Firms: A European Perspective*. Basingstoke: Palgrave MacMillan.

Cortzen, Jan (1996), *LEGO-manden—historien om Godtfred Kirk Kristiansen*. Köpenhamn: Børsens förlag.

Dagens Industri, Weekend, "Härifrån till evigheten", 31 December 2015.

Dagens Nyheter, "Bonnier tar över TV4", 22 mars 2007, signerad Andreas Cervenka.

The Danfoss Story (2010).

De Geer, Hans (1998), *Firman: familj och företagande under 125 år: Från A Johnson & Co till Axel Johnson gruppen*. Stockholm: Atlantis.

Donner, Jörn (1991), *Fazer 100*. Helsingfors: Söderström & Co Förlagsaktiebolag.

Ds (1992), Arbetsmarknadsdepartementet, "Gnosjöfenomenet", 91.

Economist (2016), "A Nordic Pyramid: The Lessons from 100 Years of a Family's Industrial Empire", 12 March 2016.

Ekegren, Bo (1994), *Lundbergs 1944–1994—en jubileumskrönika*.

Ellemose, Søren (2004), *Århundredets stjerne. A.P. Møller—Mærsk Gruppen 1904–2004*. København: Handelshøjskolens Forlag.

Ericson, Bengt (1982), *Johnsons. Den sista dynastin*. Stockholm: Affärsförlaget.

Ericson, Bengt (2007), *Antonias revansch*. Stockholm: Fischer & Co.

Family Business Yearbook (2014).

Family Business Yearbook (2015).

Fellman, Susanna and Hans Sjögren (2008), "Conclusion", in: Susanna Fellman, Marin Iversen, Hans Sjögren and Lars Thue (eds.), *Creating Nordic Capitalism: The History of a Competitive Periphery*. London: Palgrave MacMillan.

Fernández Pérez, Paloma and Andrea Lluch (eds.) (2016), *Evolution of Family Business: Continuity and Change in Latin America and Spain*. Cheltenham: Edward Elgar.

Fødselsdagsinterview med Bitten Clausen 2012 i anledning af hendes 100-års fødselsdag, af Gertraudt Jepsen.

Glete, Jan (1994), *Nätverk i näringslivet*. Stockholm: SNS Förlag.

Grundfos (1992), *Poul Due Jensen—manden, der skabte Grundfos*. Grundfos Management.

Gulbrandsen, Trygve and Even Lange (2009), "The Survival of Family Dynasties in Shipping." *International Journal of Maritime History*, 21(1): 175–200.

Håkansson, Håkan and Jan Johanson (eds.) (2001), *Business Network Learning*. Oxford: Pergamon.

Hall, Annika and Mattias Nordqvist (2008), "Professional Management in Family Businesses: Toward an Extended Understanding." *Family Business Review*, 21(1): 51–69.

Hansen, Ole Steen (1997), *LEGO och Godtfred Kirk Kristiansen*. Malmö: Bokfabriken fakta.

Hauge, Odd Harald (1993), *Fred. Olsen. Uautoriserat biografi*. Olso: Gyldendal Norsk Forlag.

Henrekson, Magnus (1996), *Företagandets villkor. Spelregler för sysselsättning och tillväxt*. Stockholm: SNS Förlag.

Herranen, Timo (2015), *Family Business, Faucet Company, Industrial Owner: Oras 1945–2015*. Helsinki: Otava Publishing Company.

Hornby, O. (1988), *Ved rettidig Omhu. Skibsreder A. P. Møller 1876–1965*. Köpenhamn: Schultz forlag.

Hoving, Victor (1951), *Karl Fazer 1891–1951*. Helsingfors.

Hufvudstadsbladet (13 June 2009), "Släkten Herlin en av Finlands rikaste", signed by Staffan Bruun.

Interview of Hans Brindfors (30 September 2016).

Iversen, Martin Jes and Steen Andersen (2008), "Co-Operative Liberalism: Denmark from 1857 to 2007", in: Fellman Susanna, Iversen, Martin, Sjögren, Hans and Lars Thue (eds.), *Creating Nordic Capitalism: The Business History of a Competitive Periphery*. Palgrave MacMillan.

Jaffe, Dennis and Sam Lane (2004), "Sustaining a Family Dynasty: Key Issues Facing Complex Multigenerational Business- and Investment-Owning Families." *Family Business Review*, 13(1).

James, Harold (2006), *Family Capitalism*. Cambridge, MA: Harvard University Press.

James, Harold (2013), "Family Values or Crony Capitalism?", in: Andrea Colli and Paloma Fernández Pérez (eds.), *The Endurance of Family Businesses: A Global Overview*. Cambridge: Cambridge University Press.

Jephson, Chris and Henning Morgen (2014), *Maersk Line. Globale muligheder og udfordringer 1973–2013*. Köpenhamn: Gyldendal Business.

Johannisson, Bengt (2012), "Familjeföretagande—en livsform för alla tider?", in: Brundin et al. (eds.), *Familjeföretagande. Affärer och känslor*. Stockholm: SNS Förlag.

Journalisten (3 April 2007), "Bonniers köp av TV4 är ett avtalsbrott", signerad Petter Larsson.

Karlsson Stider, Annelie (2000), *Familjen & Firman*. Stockholm: EFI, Handelshögskolan. Diss.

Komulainen, Anitra and Sakari Siltala (2016), "How to Build a Business Dynasty: A Comparative Study of the Business Families Ehrnrooth and Wallenberg", conference paper, EBHA, Bergen.

Kontio, Erkki and Lars von Bonsdorff (1969), *G. A. Serlachius Oy 1868–1968. Ett familjeföretags öden*.

Kristoffersson, Sara (2014), *Design by IKEA: A Cultural History*. London: Bloomsbury Academic.

Landes, David (2007), *Dynastier: De stora familjeföretagen och deras mer eller mindre lyckade affärer*. Stockholm: SNS Förlag.

Larsson, Mats (2001), *Bonniers—en mediefamilj. Förlag, konglomerat och mediekoncern 1953–1990*. Stockholm: Bonnier.

Larsson, Mats (2006), "Succession och nätverk. Bonnierföretagen i media och industri 1942–1990", in: Ylva Hasselberg and Tom Petersson (eds.), *'Bäste broder!' Nätverk, entreprenörskap och innovation i svenskt näringsliv*. Hedemora: Gidlunds.

Lindgren, Håkan (2007), *Jacob Wallenberg 1892–1980*. Stockholm: Atlantis.

Lindgren, Håkan (2012), "The Long Term Viability of the Wallenberg Family Business Group: The Role of 'a Dynastic Drive'", in: Anders Perlinge and Hans Sjögren (eds.), *Biographies in the Financial World*. Hedemora: Gidlunds.

Lubinski, Christina, Jeffrey Fear and Paloma Fernández Pérez (eds.) (2016), *Family Multinationals: Entrepreneurship, Governance and Pathways to Internationalization*. New York: Routledge.

Lumpkin, G.T., Keith H. Brigham and Todd W. Moss (2010), "Long-Term Orientation: Implications for the Entrepreneurial Orientation and Performance of Family Business" *Entrepreneurship & Regional Development*, 22(3–4): 241–64.

Lunde, Niels (2012), *Miraklet i LEGO*. Köpenhamn: Jyllands-Postens Forlag.

Magretta, Joan (1998), "Governing the Family-Owned Enterprise: An Interview with Finland's Krister Ahlström." *Harvard Business Review*, January–February Issue, pp. 113–23.

Mann, Thomas (1901), *Buddenbrooks—Verfall einer Familie*. Frankfurt am Main: S. Fisher Verlag.

Mattsson, Algot (1984), *Huset Broström. En dynastis uppgång och fall*. Göteborg: Tre böcker.

McKinsey Global Institute (January 2017) "Measuring the Economic Impact of Short-Termism".

Miller, Danny and Isabelle Le Breton-Miller (2005), *Managing for the Long Run: Lessons in Competitive Advantage from Great Family Businesses*. Boston: Harvard Business School Press.

Morck, Randall (ed.) (2005), *A History of Corporate Governance around the World: Family Business Groups to Professional Managers*. Chicago: University of Chicago Press.

Nikander, G. (1929), *Fiskars Bruks Historia*. Minnesskrift utgiven av Fiskars aktiebolag. Åbo.

Nilsson, Göran B. (2001), *Grundaren. André Oscar Wallenberg (1816–1886)*. Stockholm: Carlsson.

Nilsson, Göran B. (2005), *The Founder: André Oscar Wallenberg (1816–1886), Swedish Banker, Politician and Journalist*. Stockholm: Almqvist & Wiksell.

Nordlund, Therese (2006), "Att se det möjliga i det omöjliga. Axel Ax:son Johnson och Johnsonkoncernen", in: Ylva Hasselberg and Tom Petersson (eds.), *'Bäste broder'. Nätverk, entreprenörskap och innovation i svenskt näringsliv*. Stockholm: Gidlunds förlag.

Nordqvist, Mattias (2016), "Nu är familjeföretag 'Big Business' igen." *Företagshistoria*, Nr. 1. Stockholm.

Norland, Anders (2011a), *Bly blir gull. Schibstedts historie 1839–1933*. Oslo: Schibsted forlag.

Norland, Anders (2011b), *Medier, makt og millioner. Schibstedts historie 1934–2011*. Oslo: Schibsted forlag.

Ojala, Jari and Kalle Pajunen (2006), "Two Finnish Family Firms in Comparison: Ahlström and Schauman during the 20th Century", in: Juha-Antti Lamberg, Juha Näsi, Jari Ojala and Pasi Sajasalo (eds.), *The Evolution of Competitive Strategies in Global Forestry Industries: Comparative Perspectives*. World Forests Vol. 4. Dordrecht: Springer.

Olsson, Ulf (2000), *Att förvalta sitt pund. Marcus Wallenberg 1899–1982*. Stockholm: Ekerlids Förlag.

Olsson, Ulf (2004), *En länk i kedjan. Marc 'Boy-boy' Wallenberg 1924–1971.* Stockholm: Stiftelsen för Ekonomisk Historisk Forskning inom Bank och Företagande.

Olsson, Ulf (2006), *Finansfursten. K. A. Wallenberg 1853–1938.* Stockholm: Atlantis.

Pearson, Allison, Jon Carr and John Shaw (2008), "Towards a Theory of Familiness: A Social Capital Perspective." *Entrepreneurship Theory and Practice*, 32(6): 949–69.

Pettersson, Bo (2001), *HandelsMännen. Så skapade Erling och Stefan Persson sitt modeimperium.* Stockholm: Ekerlids Förlag.

Piketty, Thomas (2015), *Kapitalet i tjugoförsta århundradet.* Stockholm: Karneval förlag.

Rose, Mary (ed.) (1995), *Family Business.* Aldershot: Edward Elgar.

Rydenfelt, Sven (1995), *Sagan om Tetra.* Stockholm: Fischer & Co.

Sandberg, Lars (1979), "The Case of the Impoverished Sophisticate: Human Capital and Swedish Economic Growth before World War I." *Journal of Economic History*, 39(1): 225–41.

Schybergson, Per (1992), *Verk och dagar: Ahlströms historia 1851–1981.* Helsingfors.

Sejersted, Francis (2002), *Fra Linderud til Eidsvold Værk 1795–1895. En studie i industrielt gjennombrudd.* Oslo: Pax forlag.

Sjögren, Hans (1999), *Spelet i Saléninvest.* Stockholm: Ekerlids Förlag.

Sjögren, Hans (2007), *Kapitalismens värdekontrakt och relationskapital.* Stockholm: Norstedts.

Sjögren, Hans (2008), "Welfare Capitalism: The Swedish Economy 1850–2005", in: Fellman Susanna, Iversen, Martin, Sjögren, Hans and Lars Thue (eds.), *Creating Nordic Capitalism: The History of a Competitive Periphery.* London: Palgrave MacMillan.

Sjögren, Hans (2012), *Den uthålliga kapitalismen. Bolagsstyrningen i Astra, Stora Kopparbergs Berg och Svenska Tändsticksaktiebolaget.* Stockholm: SNS Förlag. Second edition.

Sjögren, Hans (2013), "Entrepreneurial Spirit in the Evolution of Swedish Family Businesses", in: Andrea Colli and Paloma Fernández Pérez (eds.), *The Endurance of Family Businesses: A Global Overview.* Cambridge: Cambridge University Press.

Sjögren, Hans (2015), *Högtryck. SAS och omvandlingen.* Stockholm: Dialogos.

Sogner, Knut (2001), *Plankeadel. Kiær- og Solberg-familien under den 2. industrielle revolusjon.* Oslo: Andresen & Butenschøn.

Sogner, Knut (2012), *Andresens. En familie i norsk økonomi og samfunnsliv gjennom to hundre år.* Oslo: Pax forlag.

SOU (2004), 39.

Stenebo, Johan (2009), *Sanningen om Ikea.* Västerås: ICA.

Sundin, Staffan (2002), *Konsolidering och expansion 1930–1954. Bonniers—en mediefamilj.* Stockholm: Albert Bonniers förlag.

SvD (26 May 2014), signed by Peter Alestig.

SvD Näringsliv (6 April 2017), "Fredrik Lundberg för över makten till sin dotter", signed by Carolina Neurath.

SvD Näringsliv (29 July 2002), "Ehrnrooths har format dagens Finland", signed by Mats Hallgren.

Sveriges radio (19 April 2005), signed by Bengt Lindroth.

Taudal Poulsen, René, Hans Sjögren and Thomas Taro Lennerfors (2012), "The Two Declines If Swedish Shipping", in: Stig Tenold, Martin Iversen and Even Lange (eds.), *Global Shipping in Small Nations*. London: Palgrave MacMillan.

Thue, Lars (2008), "Norway: a resource-based and democratic capitalism", in: Susanna Fellman, Martin Iversen, Hans Sjögren and Lars Thue (eds.), *Creating Nordic Capitalism: The History of a Competitive Periphery*. London: Palgrave MacMillan.

Torekull, Bertil (2006), *Historien om Ikea: Ingvar Kamprad berättar för Bertil Torekull*. Stockholm: Wahlström and Widstrand.

Torekull, Bertil (2011), *Kamprads lilla gulblå*. Stockholm: Ekerlids förlag.

Ward, John L. (2004), *Perpetuating the Family Business*. Basingstoke: Palgrave MacMillan.

Wennberg et al. (2011), "Implications of Intra-Family and External Ownership Transfer of Family Firms: Short-Term and Long-Term Performance Differences." *Strategic Entrepreneurship Journal*, 5: 352–72.

Wetterberg, Gunnar (2013), *Wallenberg. Ett familjeimperium*. Stockholm: Albert Bonniers förlag.

www.fazergroup.com.

Zhang, Lihua, Hans Sjögren and Miki Kishida (2016), "The Emergence and Organisational Persistence of Business Groups in China, Japan and Sweden." *Industrial and Corporate Change*, 25(6): 885–902.

Zellweger, Thomas Markus, Robert Nason and Mattias Nordqvist (2012), "From Longevity of Firms to Transgenerational Entrepreneurship of Families: Introducing Family Entrepreneurial Orientation." *Family Business Review*, 25(2): 136–55.

Index of Companies, Foundations and Individuals